To the memory of
Dr. M. R. DeHaan
Whose pastoral preaching and prophetic ministry
have impacted me even though we never met

CONTENTS

PREFACE

It is not a particularly large valley. It is a triangle that measures fifteen miles by fifteen miles by twenty miles. Yet the entire population of the world could stand in this valley without any person touching another. It is called the Valley of Armageddon, and it will be the site of the final battle of human history.

Looking over the valley from the top of Mount Carmel is a breathtaking and sobering view. It was on this mountain that Elijah defeated the prophets of Baal and God sent down fire from heaven. In this same place, the armies of the world will gather together with the objective of annihilating the Jewish people and the State of Israel. That will be Satan's last attempt in a long series of strategies to eliminate the people who are the "apple of God's eye."

The invading armies will very likely consist of a coalition of Arab-Islamic states and a massive Eastern army—perhaps Chinese—of 200 million soldiers. Initially, Israel will be defended by a Western European coalition, but at the last minute the Europeans will betray Israel. As the armies advance into the Valley of Armageddon, the destruction of the Jews seems imminent.

Then it happens—the greatest prophetic event since the birth of Jesus.

Jesus will return with the armies of heaven to destroy the armies of Satan and deliver Israel. In Elijah's day, fire fell from heaven. In the last days, Jesus himself returns from heaven. He will then establish his kingdom for one thousand years.

The Valley of Armageddon was once considered the exact center of the ancient world. Europe, Asia, and Africa all met here. More wars have been fought in this valley than anywhere else in the world. The Jews, Canaanites, Midianites, Eygptians, Syrians,

Greeks, Babylonians, Romans, Arabs, Crusaders, Turks, and British have fought and died here. The soil is soaked with their blood. And at the end of the world it will once again be the center of attention and once again reek with the blood of invading armies.

There is an eerie feeling as I gaze over the valley. Israeli jets and helicopters land at an airstrip down below. Carmelite monks chant their anthems and say their prayers behind me. Tourists from a variety of countries take photographs. Coneys sun themselves on the rocks next to the cactus. Farmers till their fields. Mountains rise to the sky in every direction. Yet this valley, which barely a century ago was just a mosquito swamp, will host "the battle of all battles."

Standing there in the warm sun, I wondered, *How close are we to Armageddon?* As we approach the year 2000, this question looms larger in the minds of many people. This book is an attempt to provide an answer. At no other time since Jesus ascended to heaven have so many remarkable events and trends come together—events and trends predicted in the Bible to be features of the end times.

How close are we? Closer than you may think!

Ed Dobson
On Mount Carmel,
overlooking the Valley of Armageddon

Chapter 1

The End of the World as We Know It

Where were you when you first heard the Beatles? Most of us who grew up in the sixties can remember distinctly where we were and what we were doing. I was at my aunt and uncle's house outside Belfast, Northern Ireland. I was playing with my cousins when we were called into the living room to see this "new" music group perform on television.

Where were you when President Kennedy was assassinated? Even though I was not an American and was still living in my native Ireland, the day is forever etched in my memory. My mom and dad had gone out for the evening, and my favorite aunt, Aunt May, was staying with us. We heard the shocking news on BBC radio. I was stunned.

For my generation, the music of the Beatles and the assassination of President Kennedy were defining moments. For me, there was still another: the Cuban missile crisis. The crisis began in the summer of 1962 with rumors about increased activity by the Soviet Union in Cuba, one of the ideological allies of the U.S.S.R. On August 29, President Kennedy ordered periodic reconnaissance flights over Cuba to monitor the shipment of military equipment. On October 14, a U–2 plane photographed two medium-range ballistic missile sites under construction. These sites could easily launch a nuclear attack against Washington, D.C., since Cuba is a mere ninety miles from the Florida coast. In a televised address on October 22, the President called for the withdrawal of Soviet equipment and personnel from Cuba and announced a naval blockade of the island. The United States and the Soviet Union were now staring each other in the face as the rest of the world held its breath.

The next weekend, the two nations edged toward the brink of all-out war. On Saturday, October 27, a U–2 plane was shot down over Cuba. Another U–2 plane strayed into Soviet airspace; Soviet planes scrambled to intercept it, and U.S. planes scrambled to rescue it. Meanwhile, at the United Nations, Soviet officials began destroying sensitive documents, which is historically one of the first preparations for war.

On Sunday, the Soviets agreed to withdraw from Cuba on the condition that the United States would pledge not to invade Cuba. Diplomacy won the day, and on November 21 the quarantine against Cuba was lifted.

I remember one particular day in late October, at the height of the drama, when I walked with my friends from Grovenor High School to a small convenience store to buy a newspaper during lunch hour. We sat on the curb of the street to look at the paper together. The thing that captured my attention was a diagram showing potential Soviet targets in the event of a nuclear war. Fortunately, Belfast was not one of the cities identified by the experts, but we were concerned about nuclear radiation and fallout from several targets in England. We walked back to school, but for the rest of the day our minds were consumed with the possibility of nuclear war.

As I rode my bicycle home that afternoon, I realized for the first time in my young life that civilization was resting on a time bomb that could explode and destroy much of the world as we know it. I went to bed that night wondering if I would wake up the next day. But the Russian ships turned back. A superpower confrontation was avoided. Things got back to normal. I went back to studying, playing soccer, going to church, and the rest. But we were all changed a little that day. We had come face-to-face with the possibility of the end of the world, and we would live with that possibility for the rest of our lives.

These events occurred more than thirty years ago. We now approach the end of a century and the beginning of a new century and a new millennium. While the Cold War is over and the Soviet Union no longer exists, the world is no more stable than it was in the fall of 1962. In fact, many scientists and observers of the global scene are worried. There are increasing signs that suggest the long-term survival of our world is at risk. According to the report called *Global 2000 Revisited: What Shall We Do?,* the world in

> the 21st century will be more crowded, more polluted, less stable economically and sociologically, and more vulnerable to violent disruption than the world we live in now. Serious stresses involving inter-religious relations, the economy, population, resources, environment, and security loom ahead.[1]

The report cites the challenges of "AIDS and tuberculosis; nuclear, chemical and biological weapons; the global debt; migration; corruption, drug trade; and technological change" and then concludes that if "we people of earth are to avoid a massive disaster within the lifetime of our children, our most critical and urgent task is to bring forth a transformed vision of progress, one of sustainable and replicable development."[2] This prediction of "massive disaster" does not arise from some extremist or alarmist group. The *Global 2000 Report* was produced by a group of esteemed scientists who were initially commissioned by President Carter to consider the challenges that the world could confront upon entering the next century. The issues that threaten our existence are innumerable.

THE NUCLEAR THREAT

Albert Einstein was right when he said that "the unleashed power of the atom has changed everything save our modes of thinking, and we thus drift toward unparalleled catastrophe."[3] On October 29, 1939, eight men met in Washington, D.C., to discuss whether the United States government should try to "acquire the power to destroy whole cities, whole nations even, at a single blow."[4] That fateful meeting eventually led to Hiroshima and the age of nuclear weapons.

Hiroshima is a microcosm of what could and might happen. The bomb that was dropped on Hiroshima exploded at 8:15 A.M. on August 6, 1945. It was nearly 10 feet long and weighed nearly 4½ tons. Everyone within a third of a mile of the explosion was killed. Within one and a quarter miles, more than 60 percent were killed. Forty percent of the total population of the city died. Shock waves of hurricane-force winds were precipitated by the blast. Fireballs 400 meters in diameter shot up, and the temperature at ground level was 5000 degrees Celsius. Violent firestorms occurred. Of the 76,000 buildings in the city, 51,000 were totally destroyed. The fallout of radiation caused nausea, vomiting, and fever. Many died within ten days because of the fallout, and many others suffered the long-term effects of cancer and birth abnormalities.[5] This bomb was ironically nicknamed "Little Boy." According to scientists, the current worldwide nuclear arsenal has the "explosive power of a million Hiroshima bombs."[6]

It is obvious that nuclear weapons have the potential to wipe out civilization as we know it. It is no wonder that a nuclear holocaust, should one occur, has been dubbed "the human event to end all human events."[7]

From their study of Hiroshima, scientists have a reasonable understanding of what a nuclear war would be like. Based on the conditions existing in the early 1980s, if there were an all-out nuclear war, the following would very likely occur:

1. *The Human Toll*
   750 million people killed (half the population of the
      cities targeted)
   340 million seriously injured
   20 percent of urban survivors incapacitated
   33 percent of urban survivors under acute anxiety

2. *The Environmental Toll*
   Water contamination
   Radiation fallout
   Rainfall with high toxic content
   Uncontrollable fires
   Particle matters in atmosphere that would hide the sun
   Inability to grow food[8]

Thus, a nuclear war would not only kill over half of the existing population, but also render the environment unstable for living for those who survived. Everything would change forever. What has prevented such a catastrophe? Only responsible choices by human beings who control nuclear weapons. But can we expect that in the future reasonable human beings will control those weapons? No—not in view of increased terrorism worldwide and the breakup of the Soviet Union into independent nations, some of which now possess nuclear weapons. It may only be a matter of time before some fanatic terrorist or nationalist decides to use nuclear weapons to advance his cause. It could be someone from Iran or Iraq. It could be a Harvard-educated mathematician who creates a nuclear bomb rather than a letter bomb. We have more to fear from a nuclear bomber than from a Unabomber.

HOW CLOSE ARE WE TO NUCLEAR DISASTER?

The Bulletin of the Atomic Scientists keeps a doomsday clock. The hands are set to indicate either the greater likelihood of nuclear annihilation or less risk of it, depending on the current international situation. When the clock was introduced in 1947, it showed seven minutes to midnight. In 1953, it moved to two minutes to midnight when the United States tested a hydrogen bomb.

In 1963, the clock moved back to twelve minutes to midnight when the United States and the Soviet Union signed a treaty limiting the testing of nuclear weapons—the "partial test ban treaty." In 1984, it moved forward to four minutes to midnight as the two superpowers developed more nuclear capabilities. In 1991, the clock moved back to seventeen minutes to midnight with the signing of the Strategic Arms Reduction Treaty (START). The clock was last reset on December 8, 1995, moving forward to fourteen minutes before midnight. The following reasons were given for moving the clock forward:

- Four years after the signing of START, the United States and Russia collectively possess more than 35,000 nuclear weapons, strategic and tactical.
- No new arms reduction treaties are in progress. Implementation of START II and the future of the Anti-Ballistic Missile Treaty are in doubt.
- The United States government speaks of "hedging" its bets against a resurgent Russia because, in having failed to integrate Russia into the community of democratic nations, it fears an adversarial relationship is emerging.
- In Russia itself, nationalists increasingly resist the reduction of nuclear weapons as a matter of national pride.
- Beyond the borders of the United States and Russia, a few states secretly covet nuclear weapons. There is a real danger that terrorist groups might obtain nuclear weapons. More than a thousand tons of weapons—grade uranium and plutonium—enough to make tens of thousands of bombs—are stockpiled, much of it under inadequate security.
- Efforts toward eliminating chemical and biological weapons have not been ratified by the United States and Russia.

The world remains moments from nuclear disaster and the situation is getting worse—not better.

NUCLEAR BOMBS AND THE BIBLE

> But the day of the Lord will come like a thief. The heavens will disappear with a roar; the elements will be destroyed by fire, and the earth and everything in it will be laid bare.
>
> *2 Peter 3:10*

The Bible has much to say about the end of the world, and some of its predictions have incredible similarities to the scenario drawn for nuclear holocaust. Saint Peter predicts that in the last days the world will be destroyed by fire and a new heaven and a new earth will be introduced (2 Peter 3:3–13). He identifies three major characteristics of these cataclysmic events.

1. *Explosion in the heavens*
   "The heavens will disappear with a roar" (v. 10). The bomb dropped on Hiroshima did not explode on the ground. It exploded 510 meters above the center of the city.

2. *Things melting with heat*
   "The elements will melt in the heat" (v. 12). In a nuclear explosion, one-third of the total energy is given off in heat. At Hiroshima, this heat created fireballs 400 meters in diameter.

3. *Destruction of the earth*
   "The earth and everything in it will be laid bare" (v. 10). In the aftermath of nuclear holocaust, forests, grasslands, and rivers would be burned and destroyed.

The book of Revelation (also called the Apocalypse) predicts similar events at the end of the world. In chapter 8, four angels are introduced who sound four trumpets that signal an ongoing judgment upon planet Earth. First, these judgments fall from the sky. They are described as follows (vv. 6–10):

"Hail and fire, mixed with blood . . . hurled down upon the earth."

"Something like a huge mountain, all ablaze, was thrown into the sea."

"A great star, blazing like a torch, fell from the sky."

Remember, these descriptions were written nearly two thousand years ago, yet they could be used today to describe the falling of nuclear bombs. Can you see people being interviewed by CNN in the aftermath of a nuclear explosion?

"It was like hail balls of fire falling from the sky."

"I was standing on the beach, and out on the horizon it looked like a huge mountain hitting the sea. Fire everywhere."

"At first I thought it was a falling star—but falling stars don't hit the earth the way this one did."

Second, these judgments bring massive destruction to the earth (vv. 6–10):

A third of the earth burned
A third of the trees burned
All the green grass burned
A third of the sea turned to blood
A third of the sea creatures killed
A third of the rivers and waters polluted

These are similar to the consequences of a nuclear holocaust. Even the solar system would feel the effects. "A third of the day was without light, and also a third of the night." The world became dark. Scientists call it "twilight at noon"—the accumulation of dark particle matter that absorbs and reflects light. This phenomenon results in obscuring the light of the sun.[9]

So the world would become burned, charred, polluted, poisoned, and dark in a nuclear holocaust—exactly what is predicted in the Bible.

BEYOND THE BOMB

Nuclear annihilation is certainly the most urgent threat in regard to the end of the world, but it is not the only one. Beyond the bomb, many other factors cause scientists to question the survivability of the world as we know it.

1. *Population explosion along with reduced food supply*

Every year the population of the world increases by more than 90 million people. Seventy years ago, the rate was 15 million per year. We will not be able to feed the growing world population indefinitely. According to a report of the Millennium Institute on June 28, 1996, there were then 5,770,840,831 people in the world. Given the current population growth rate, we will soon run out of enough land to grow the needed amounts of food. If people are fed a "northern" diet (as in the United States, Canada, and Europe), "humanity would run out of enough available land to grow food to feed everyone in 9 years. This is assuming all potentially available land is used and no land is held aside for species conservation, preservation of wilderness, etc."[10] If one calculates available land by current use, the world "passed the point where it could feed everyone a 'northern' diet in 1987."[11]

With these limited resources, the stage is being set for conflict between the rich and the poor as well as famines of global proportions. Famine would no longer be confined to the shores of Somalia or the refugee camps of the Sudan. The book of Revelation predicts such worldwide famine as we approach the end of the world.

> When the Lamb opened the third seal, I heard the third living creature say, "Come!" I looked, and there before me was a black horse! Its rider was holding a pair of scales in his hand. Then I heard what sounded like a voice among the four living creatures, saying, "A quart of wheat for a day's wages, and three quarts of barley for a day's wages, and do not damage the oil and the wine."   *Revelation 6:5–6*

2. *Disease*

For several years I have served with the World Council of Churches in addressing the pandemic of HIV/AIDS. I have worked with a small group of Christians from around the world to forge a document that would help churches address this global problem. I remember the time we spent in Geneva with officers of the World Health Organization (WHO) and heard from people of many nations. The magnitude of the HIV/AIDS problem is overwhelming. WHO estimated that by mid-1994, more than 4 million people worldwide were infected with HIV viruses, with 60 percent of the cases being in sub-Sahara Africa. Seventy percent of the infections came from heterosexual contacts. It is estimated that by the year 2000, more than 40 million people will be infected.[12]

HIV/AIDS may be a harbinger of future global struggles with other sickness and disease. Doctors in the Western world are concerned that common viruses are becoming resistant to traditional antibiotics. The threat of a disease fatal to humans but spread by cows sent shock waves through Europe in the mid-nineties. In a world of advanced medical knowledge and ongoing research for chemical cures, diseases still wreak havoc all over the world. The book of Revelation predicts such challenges as we approach the end of the age.

> When the Lamb opened the fourth seal, I heard the voice of the fourth living creature say, "Come!" I looked, and there before me was a pale horse! Its rider was named Death, and Hades was following close behind him. They were given power over a fourth of the earth to kill by sword, famine and plague, and by the wild beasts of the earth. *Revelation 6:7–8*

Now, can you imagine what would happen if a nation launched even a small biological warhead? In 1960 the head of the U.S. Army Chemical Corps stated that an enemy could "kill or seriously disable 30 percent of the American population—about sixty million people—by mounting a biological warfare attack with only ten aircraft."[13]

3. *Poisoning the environment and the misuse of natural resources*

Have we forgotten the nuclear accident at Chernobyl in the Ukraine in 1986? Scientists estimate that the disaster could eventually result in 10,000 deaths by cancer. Have we forgotten the toxic gas leak in Bhopal, India, in 1984? More than 2,500 people were killed and 150,000 injured. Environmental disasters continue. Consider the following facts from *Racing Toward 2001:*

More than 700 chemicals have been detected in U.S.
    drinking water.
About 20 billion tons of waste end up in the seas each year.
Forest destruction has brought on widespread flooding and
    loss of topsoil, has contributed to global warming, and
    has speeded the extinction of plants and animals.
Each person in the United States generates an average of
    almost a ton of trash each year.[14]

The Millennium Institute predicts the following environmental challenges:[15]

Species extinction per day	104
Years until a third of species are lost	10
Years until half of crude oil is gone	4
Years until carbon dioxide doubles	61

So what does the future hold? Remember, we are not quot-
ing the Bible here, but modern scientists: poisoned water to drink,
the extinction of many species, global warming, consumption of
natural resources, destruction of forests, pollution of lakes and
streams and oceans, continued natural and technological catastro-
phes. Again, these hold incredible parallels to the predictions of
the book of Revelation. The Bible predicts the pollution of the sea
and the death of one-third of sea creatures (Revelation 8:8), the
death of human beings from polluted waters (v. 11), and the
destruction of forests and grasslands (v. 7).

THE END OF THE WORLD: AN OVERVIEW

Students of global trends paint a bleak and dark picture for
the future of our world. It would be a world with

The increasing possibility of nuclear disaster that would
    end civilization as we know it.
The inability to feed its people, leading to famine and war.
A natural environment that will struggle to sustain life,
    with the air and water polluted, the food supply
    poisoned, and the ozone layer depleted.

Plagues that medical science cannot control or cure.

When we turn to the Bible, we discover these same kinds of descriptions, though not in the same amount of detail.

The potential (or reality) of nuclear destruction (Revelation 8:6–12; 2 Peter 3:10–12)
Worldwide famine (Revelation 6:5–6)
Pollution of the environment (Revelation 8:6–12)
Plagues (Revelation 6:7–8)

More broadly speaking, the Bible has a great deal to say about the global conditions that will prevail as the end of the world as we know it approaches. Later on, I identify and examine fifty remarkable events and trends that are predicted in the Bible about the end times. I believe that we could indeed be living in the last days and that we are close to the end. My belief is based on the following major propositions that form the core of this book:

1. The Bible predicts that Jesus will come back to the earth.
2. The Bible predicts the specific events and trends that will precede and accompany the coming of Jesus.
3. The current situation in the world has remarkable parallels to the events and trends predicted in the Bible.

THE TOUGH MORAL QUESTIONS

If we are living in the last days (and even if we are not), how should we respond to these biblical predictions and their apparent fulfillment in present-day events? What about the threat of nuclear war? What about the plight of those who are hungry? What about the multitudes infected with HIV and AIDS? What about the poisoning of our environment and the extinction of species? Should we care about any of this? Herein lies our moral dilemma.

Some Christians appear excited about all these events. They seem to have the attitude, "Push the nuclear button. Get it over with. Let God sort it out." Should we be happy about "bad news" that portends "good news"? Other Christians dismiss altogether the prophetic implications of Scripture. They sometimes accuse us who take these predictions literally as obscurantists who ignore the realities of the world in which we live. They say our obsession with the "end times" is an emotional cop-out from dealing with the tough questions posed by cultural and social conditions. Is it? How should we respond?

How close are we to the end of the world? Could Jesus return before A.D. 2000? And how should Christians respond to these issues? These are questions that many people are asking. I hope they will all be addressed to your satisfaction within the pages of this book.

Chapter 2

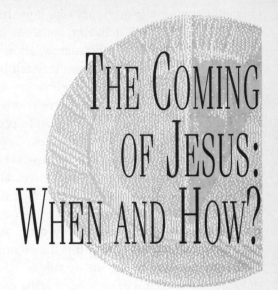

THE COMING OF JESUS: WHEN AND HOW?

"At that time the sign of the Son of Man will appear in the sky, and all the nations of the earth will mourn. They will see the Son of Man coming on the clouds of the sky, with power and great glory. And he will send his angels with a loud trumpet call, and they will gather his elect from the four winds, from one end of the heavens to the other."

Matthew 24:30–31

Christopher Reeve was the ultimate Superman. The actor had the looks, the language, and the screen presence to be what the world is looking for and desperately needs—the superhero who can right all wrongs and conquer all evil plans. He is stronger than a locomotive, faster than a speeding bullet, and able to leap tall buildings. He looks like one of us, but when he changes clothes he transcends the limitations of human flesh. "It's a bird! It's a plane! It's Superman!"

One reason why Superman fascinates us is that this fictional character connects to our inner longings. In a world of injustice and evil, we long for a deliverer, someone who can stop the evil and correct the wrong. Unfortunately, all our human heroes have feet of clay, and none of them can leap tall buildings. So we keep watching Superman movies and television reruns in the hope that maybe one day our fantasy will become reality.

In fact, one day it will! The Bible predicts the coming of Jesus Christ to set up his kingdom. Like Superman, he looks like one of us, but he is distinctly different—he is the Son of God, and when he comes he will indeed stop evil, establish justice, and correct the wrong. Ever since the fall of Adam and Eve in the Garden of Eden and the resultant sickness, decay, and death, God has been about the plan of redeeming creation and human beings through his Son, Jesus Christ. It is the coming of Jesus—the first time to suffer, the second time to rule as King—that offers hope of Paradise regained. The coming of Jesus and the end of the world are part of God's larger plan for humanity and creation.

THE BEGINNING—A VERY GOOD PLACE TO START

In the beginning God created the heavens and the earth.
Genesis 1:1

The opening verse of the Bible establishes two foundational theological truths. First, God exists. Second, the God who exists created the world. The verb *created* (in the Hebrew, *bara*) means to produce or generate something. It is used exclusively of God in the Old Testament—never in connection with the work of human beings. Theologians describe this act of creation as *ex nihilo,* "out of nothing." Louis Berkhof defines creation as "that free act of God whereby He, according to His sovereign will and for His own glory, in the beginning brought forth the whole visible and invisible universe, without the use of pre-existent material, and thus gave it an existence, distinct from His own and yet always dependent on Him."[1]

After this initial announcement, the Bible describes God's creative activity day by day, explaining each day with a similar language and structure. This structure centers around three phrases in the text.

"God said"
"It was so"
"It was good"

After six days, the work of creation was completed. The Bible gives God's evaluation of what he had created, including human beings.

> God saw all that he had made, and it was very good. And there was evening, and there was morning—the sixth day. *Genesis 1:31*

The word *good* (in the Hebrew, *tob*) refers not only to the perfection of God's creation, but also to its beneficial qualities. The world God had created was good and beneficial for the human beings he placed in that world to care for it. God knew what was best and good for human beings. The tragedy of the Fall is that Adam and Eve rejected their Creator's good and sought their own good.

> When the woman saw that the fruit of the tree was good for food and pleasing to the eye, and also desirable for gaining wisdom, she took some and ate it. She also gave some to her husband, who was with her, and he ate it. *Genesis 3:6*

On the sixth day God created Adam and then Eve. When they were placed in the Garden of Eden, they had an intimate relationship with God and with each other and a positive relationship with their environment. They walked with God and talked with him in the cool of the day. They cared for the garden and enjoyed the fruit of the trees. There were "both naked, and they felt no shame" (Genesis 2:25). They had an open, honest, vulnerable relationship with each other. They had nothing to hide—no games, no masks, no roles, no acting, no dysfunctions. This was God's creative purpose: a world in harmony with itself and human beings, human beings in harmony with each other and their Creator, a true Paradise. The creation was "very good" (Genesis 1:31).

THE FALL—PARADISE LOST

The intimacy of Eden did not last. Adam and Eve chose to disregard God's word and listened to the voice of Satan, the archenemy of God. Two things immediately happened. First, Adam and Eve's intimacy with each other was broken.

> Then the eyes of both of them were opened, and they realized they were naked; so they sewed fig leaves together and made coverings for themselves.   *Genesis 3:7*

They began hiding from each other by sewing fig leaves together. They started building walls between each other.

Second, their intimacy with God was shattered, and they started hiding from God.

> Then the man and his wife heard the sound of the LORD God as he was walking in the garden in the cool of the day, and they hid from the LORD God among the trees of the garden.   *V. 8*

And so goes the history of the human race—alienated from God and from each other. God confronted Adam and Eve and the serpent that had tempted them, and he pronounced judgment on all three. Two key ideas permeated the conversation of God. First is the idea of conflict; second, the idea of pain that is associated with the conflict. God makes three critical statements about the world as it came to be in the aftermath of the Fall.

1. *It would be a world of perpetual conflict between good and evil.*

> So the LORD God said to the serpent, "Because you have done this,
>
> *"Cursed are you above all the livestock*
> *and all the wild animals!*
> *You will crawl on your belly*
> *and you will eat dust*

> *all the days of your life.*
> *And I will put enmity*
>   *between you and the woman,*
>   *and between your offspring and hers;*
> *he will crush your head,*
>   *and you will strike his heel."*
>
> *Vv. 14–15*

God foretold that the history of the human race would be one of perpetual conflict—enmity—between Satan and his demons on the one hand and the woman and her descendants on the other. God also predicted that pain would be a part of the conflict. Satan would "strike the heel," and the seed of the woman would "crush" the serpent's head.

2. *It would be a world of perpetual conflict between men and women.*

To the woman he said,

> *"I will greatly increase your pains in childbearing;*
>   *with pain you will give birth to children.*
> *Your desire will be for your husband,*
>   *and he will rule over you."*
>
> *V. 16*

As a result of sin, the woman would experience pain in the process of childbearing. Her "desire" for her husband carries the idea of a yearning to control or dominate. It is used to describe sin that desires to master us (Genesis 4:7). "Your desire will be for your husband" could also be translated "your desire to control and dominate will be against your husband." The husband's response is to dominate as well: "he will rule over you." One consequence of the Fall is gender conflict—men and women naturally seek to control and dominate each other.

3. *It would be a world of perpetual conflict between humans and creation.*

To Adam he said, "Because you listened to your wife and ate from the tree about which I commanded you, 'You must not eat of it,'

> *"Cursed is the ground because of you;*
> *through painful toil you will eat of it*
> *all the days of your life.*
> *It will produce thorns and thistles for you,*
> *and you will eat the plants of the field.*
> *By the sweat of your brow*
> *you will eat your food*
> *until you return to the ground,*
> *since from it you were taken;*
> *for dust you are*
> *and to dust you will return."*
>
> *Vv. 17–19*

The environment would not be user friendly for Adam, but would continually work against him. Just existing would be "painful toil." After living a life dominated by the "sweat of the brow," he would die and go back to dust.

The harmony that existed in creation prior to the Fall had been disrupted. Adam and Eve were now living in a new world. Pain, disease, conflict, sorrow, frustration, and death were part of their new reality. Saint Paul elaborates on this reality in chapter 8 of his letter to the Romans. First, he declares that "the creation was subjected to frustration" (Romans 8:20). The word *frustration* means an inability to reach one's goal. It means to go fishing and never catch a fish. Creation is frustrated because it cannot reach its intended goal—harmony with itself and intimacy between human beings and God. Second, Paul states that creation is in "bondage to decay" (v. 21). Things are not getting better in the world; they are getting worse. The seeds of decay, corruption, destruction and death are sown into the fabric of the fallen creation. Third, Paul states that "the whole creation has been groaning as in the pains of childbirth right up to the present time" (v. 22). Creation longs to be delivered from the curse and consequences of sin.

A GLIMMER OF HOPE

The consequences of the Fall remind us of the song sung on the television program *Hee Haw.*

Gloom, despair and agony on me,
deep dark depression, excessive misery.

We are in fact broken-down people living in a broken-down world. The Fall brought a series of realities that cannot be avoided.

1. *Conflict is a part of life*. There is no such a thing as a life devoid of conflict. We live in a war zone between good and evil. We forge human relationships with a bent toward domination and control. We fight the forces of nature to earn a living.

This conflict is not confined to human relationships. It is played out at the national and international level as human authorities seek to dominate and control each other. On September 4, 1996, the day I wrote this chapter, I went to one of my favorite delis for lunch. As I waited to be served, I glanced at the headlines of *The Wall Street Journal*. Under the World-Wide News section there were thirteen major news headlines, and most of them dealt with conflict and war.[2]

THE U.S. ATTACKED Iraq with cruise missiles, and further strikes are possible. The 27 missiles, fired from B–52 bombers and warships in the Persian Gulf, struck targets in southern Iraq. Iraqi officials said five people died.

Yeltsin approved a peace treaty with Chechen separatist rebels, according to Prime Minister Chernomyrdin, but opposition to the pact negotiated by national security chief Lebed grew among Communists in the Duma. Lebed told a news conference 90,000 have died in the war, but gave no evidence.

U.N. refugee officials began evacuating 31 Muslims from the Bosnian city of Banja Luka after an angry mob of Serbs evicted them from their homes.

Hutu rebels in Burundi fired mortar rounds into Bujumbura, causing no injuries but marking their first attack on the capital this year and the first since a coup by the Tutsi-led army in July. Fighting continued around the northern city of Kayanza, where rebels began an offensive last week. An army spokesman said casualties are high.

Israeli negotiators continued discussions with Palestinian officials in an effort to arrange the first meeting between Netanyahu and Arafat and rekindle the peace process.

The administration plans to reassign 500 FBI agents to the bureau's counterterrorism force as it investigates suspected terrorist bombings in Saudi Arabia and Atlanta and the July 17 explosion of TWA 747.

The IRS is conducting an audit of a course House Speaker Gingrich taught for two years, officials at two Georgia colleges said.

Colombia unveiled a plan to require individuals or businesses with a net worth of more than $85,000 to buy war bonds to help finance Bogota's war against leftist rebels.

Belgian police found the remains of two teenage girls who were the subject of an intense manhunt involving a suspected ring of murderous child pornographers centered in the city of Charleroi.

Pakistan said it has shot down four Indian helicopters in recent weeks in a border dispute over a glacier in the mountainous region north of Kashmir.

Sri Lanka's military said it has arrested a Tamil separatist rebel it believes was one of the people who placed bombs on a crowded commuter train in a suburb of Colombo, the capital, in July. The explosions killed at least 57 people and wounded more than 500.

Rescue workers in India searched for more victims of a Bombay building collapse that killed at least six people.

Ethiopian merchants marched in Addis Ababa to protest rent increases by the government on state-owned properties, where some 21,000 shops are located.

2. *Dealing with conflict demands hard work.* It takes work to resist evil. It takes work to cultivate intimate and meaningful relationships with others. It takes work to survive in a hostile world. The Bible calls it "painful toil."

3. *Pain is part of the deal.* Sometimes we experience the pain of Satan "striking" the heel. Sometimes it is the pain of birthing and rearing children. Sometimes it is the pain of broken relationships and the hurt of others. Sometimes it is the pain of working hard. But there is always pain. And when we come to the end of the journey, there is the ultimate pain—the pain of dying.

Against the darkness of these realities there is a rainbow of hope. As God conversed with Satan, Eve, and Adam, he offered a promise.

> *"And I will put enmity*
>   *between you and the woman,*
>   *and between your offspring and hers;*
> *he will crush your head,*
>   *and you will strike his heel."*
>
> Genesis 3:15

God predicted that the seed of the woman—a reference to the promised Messiah (Galatians 3:16; Revelation 12:1–5)—would "crush"—deal a fatal blow—to Satan. In the process, Satan would harm—though not fatally—the promised Messiah. Theologians call this verse the *protevangelium,* the "first gospel." God predicted that someone born of a woman would eventually defeat the forces of Satan and evil. This promise becomes the theme of the entire Bible and culminates with the judgment of Satan.

> And the devil, who deceived them, was thrown into the lake of burning sulfur, where the beast and the false prophet had been thrown. They will be tormented day and night for ever and ever.   *Revelation 20:10*

THE COMING OF CHRIST AS PREDICTED IN THE OLD TESTAMENT

Beginning with the *protevangelium*, the Old Testament records the working of God through the Jewish people to fulfill the promise that the seed of the woman would crush the head of the serpent. With ever-increasing detail, the Old Testament Scriptures predict the coming of this Promised One. From these predictions, two major themes emerge. First, the Promised One will come to earth and will suffer, die, and rise again. This is his first coming (or advent). Second, the Promised One will also come in glory and power to establish a kingdom of righteousness over all the earth. This is called his second coming (or advent).

The exact fulfillment of every detail of his first coming gives us confidence that every detail of his second coming will come to pass. We can trust Bible prophecy!

1. *Predictions concerning the First Coming*

The Old Testament predicted that Christ would be born of a virgin (Isaiah 7:14) in the city of Bethlehem (Micah 5:2). It predicted that he would be betrayed by a friend (Psalm 41:9) for thirty pieces of silver (Zechariah 11:12–13). It predicted that he would be subjected to shame (Isaiah 50:6), his hands pierced (Psalm 22:16), his garments parted (Psalm 22:18), and his body wounded (Isaiah 53). It predicted that he would die and make his grave with the rich (Isaiah 53:9); he would be raised from the dead (Psalm 16:10) and would ascend on high (Psalm 68:18).

These are just a few of the predictions concerning the first coming of Christ to the earth. After his resurrection, Jesus appeared to two of his disciples on the road to Emmaus and explained all the Old Testament references to his sufferings.

> He said to them, "How foolish you are, and how slow of heart to believe all that the prophets have spoken! Did not the Christ have to suffer these things and then enter his glory?" And beginning with Moses and all the Prophets, he explained to them what was said in all the Scriptures concerning himself. *Luke 24:25–27*

2. *Predictions concerning the Second Coming*

Joy to the world! the Lord is come!
Let earth receive her King;
Let ev'ry heart prepare Him room,
And heav'n and nature sing,

And heav'n and nature sing,
And heav'n, and heav'n and nature sing.

Joy to the earth! the Savior reigns!
Let men their songs employ;
While fields and floods, rocks, hills and plains
Repeat the sounding joy,
Repeat the sounding joy,
Repeat, repeat the sounding joy.

No more let sins and sorrows grow,
Nor thorns infest the ground;
He comes to make His blessings flow
Far as the curse is found,
Far as the curse is found,
Far as, far as the curse is found.

He rules the world with truth and grace,
And makes the nations prove
The glories of His righteousness
And wonders of His love,
And wonders of His love,
And wonders, wonders of His love.

We often sing this familiar carol at Christmas, which celebrates Jesus' first coming. But this hymn is really about the Second Coming. It was written by Isaac Watts and is based on several passages of Scripture, including Psalm 98.

There are many predictions in the Old Testament that focus on Christ's rule on the earth. He will come in glory, dominion, and power (Daniel 7:13–14) and will be exalted (Isaiah 2:11). He will set his feet on the Mount of Olives (Zechariah 14:4), and the Jews will look upon him (Zechariah 12:10). He will be king over all the earth (Zechariah 14:9). He will bring peace to the world (Isaiah 2:4) and will be worshiped (Zechariah 14:16). His coming will be accompanied by a day of wrath (Zephaniah 1:15). Isaiah summarized these promises of a future earthly kingdom.

Of the increase of his government and peace
there will be no end.

He will reign on David's throne
and over his kingdom,
establishing and upholding it
with justice and righteousness
from that time on and forever.
The zeal of the LORD Almighty
will accomplish this.

Isaiah 9:7

The coming of Christ to suffer (his humiliation) and the coming of Christ to reign as king (his exaltation) are two distinct themes and separate events. One event has already taken place—Christ has suffered, died, risen, and returned to the Father. The other event still awaits fulfillment—Christ's return to the earth.

THE SECOND COMING AS PREDICTED IN THE NEW TESTAMENT

The New Testament elaborates on the theme of the second coming of Jesus Christ. The eleven disciples were with Jesus when he ascended to heaven. As the disciples gazed into the sky, two angels appeared to them and promised that "This same Jesus, who has been taken from you into heaven, will come back in the same way you have seen him go into heaven" (Acts 1:11). For nearly two thousand years the followers of Jesus have cherished that hope—the hope of the literal and physical return of Christ. While Christians have disagreed on and have debated precisely how and when this will occur, they all agree that Jesus will come again.

Three Words

In the New Testament, three Greek words are used to describe the second coming of Jesus Christ. First is the word *parousia,* which comes from a verb meaning "to be near or alongside of." It is used twenty-four times in the New Testament and focuses on the bodily appearance of Christ. When he returns, we will be near him.

The second word is *apokalupsis,* from which comes the word *apocalypse,* which is the Greek title of the book of Revelation. It means "to uncover or reveal." The focus in reference to the second coming is on the revealing of Christ in his glory.

The third word is *epiphaneia*, which means "to bring forth into light." The word points up that Christ's coming will be unmistakable—as dramatic as light in the midst of darkness.

Two Stages

If Jesus is coming back to establish his kingdom, exactly how will this take place? As we study the predictions of the New Testament, two themes emerge. First, Jesus will come *for* his saints in the clouds and take them to heaven. Second, he will come *with* his saints to the earth to establish a kingdom. I believe there are two stages of his coming that are separated by a seven-year period of tribulation.

Stage one: Coming for his saints

Brothers, we do not want you to be ignorant about those who fall asleep, or to grieve like the rest of men, who have no hope. We believe that Jesus died and rose again and so we believe that God will bring with Jesus those who have fallen asleep in him. According to the Lord's own word, we tell you that we who are still alive, who are left till the coming of the Lord, will certainly not precede those who have fallen asleep. For the Lord himself will come down from heaven, with a loud command, with the voice of the archangel and with the trumpet call of God, and the dead in Christ will rise first. After that, we who are still alive and are left will be caught up together with them in the clouds to meet the Lord in the air. And so we will be with the Lord forever. Therefore encourage each other with these words.   *1 Thessalonians 4:13–18*

Note the emphasis in Christ's coming. He will descend from heaven, and we will be "caught up." This is the concept of the "Rapture." Although the word *rapture* does not occur in the New Testament, the idea does occur. We will "meet the Lord in the air."

There is no mention of Jesus' touching the earth—he comes down only as far as the clouds. We leave the earth—we do not establish a kingdom with Christ on the earth. So the rapture of the church will occur when believers are taken out of the world to meet with the Lord and stay with him.

The rapture of believers is the next great prophetic event on the calendar of God. I believe that it could come at any moment.

Stage two: Coming with his saints. The New Testament also predicts that Jesus will return to the earth with the armies of heaven, which include the saints. He will defeat Satan and establish a kingdom on the earth. John describes this prophetic event in Revelation 19:11–16.

> I saw heaven standing open and there before me was a white horse, whose rider is called Faithful and True. With justice he judges and makes war. His eyes are like blazing fire, and on his head are many crowns. He has a name written on him that no one knows but he himself. He is dressed in a robe dipped in blood, and his name is the Word of God. The armies of heaven were following him, riding on white horses and dressed in fine linen, white and clean. Out of his mouth comes a sharp sword with which to strike down the nations. "He will rule them with an iron scepter." He treads the winepress of the fury of the wrath of God Almighty. On his robe and on his thigh he has this name written: KING OF KINGS AND LORD OF LORDS.

We learn from this passage that Jesus does not come to take believers to heaven. Instead, he comes at a time when the believers are already in heaven. He does not stop in the air, but comes all the way to earth. He does not come to deliver his people from the earth, but rather, to rule with his people on the earth. The nature, purpose, and consequence of this coming are radically different from the Rapture.

The Second Coming and the Great Tribulation

Given these two stages to the second coming of Christ, the compelling question becomes, "How far apart are these two events?" The answer is seven years. Between these two stages is the seven-year period known as the Great Tribulation. This event is confirmed in the prophecies of Daniel in regard to the 490 years of future events (Daniel 9:24–27) and the structure of the book of Revelation. An analysis of both of these issues is given in later chapters.

The next major event in the prophetic calendar of God is the rapture of the church, and it could occur at any moment. After that, the Tribulation will begin with the introduction of the Antichrist, who will be aligned with a renewed economic-political Roman Empire—that is, Europe. The Antichrist will be a brilliant nego-tiator and militarist who will usher in world peace. He will forge a peace treaty to guarantee the security of Israel, but will break the treaty after three and a half years. During this time chaos will engulf the globe. There will be famines and plagues of epidemic proportions. Millions will die. The rivers and grasslands will be poisoned and burned. Events that parallel nuclear disaster will become commonplace.

The world will be influenced economically by global inter-ests. Commerce will be controlled internationally, and only those with the appropriate mark, or key, will be allowed to buy and sell. Religions will unify into a single worldwide faith. Then at the end, a coalition of armies in the Middle East will march on Israel to exterminate all the Jews. At the last moment, Christ will return with the armies of heaven to defeat this coalition at the Battle of Armageddon. With this victory he will establish the millennial kingdom on the earth. Then will come to pass this prophecy:

> *The wolf will live with the lamb,*
> *the leopard will lie down with the goat,*
> *the calf and the lion and the yearling together;*
> *and a little child will lead them.*
> *The cow will feed with the bear,*
> *their young will lie down together,*
> *and the lion will eat straw like the ox.*
> *The infant will play near the hole of the cobra,*

and the young child put his hand into the viper's nest.
They will neither harm nor destroy
   on all my holy mountain,
for the earth will be full of the knowledge of the LORD
   as the waters cover the sea.

Isaiah 11:6–9

LET'S GO BACK TO THE BEGINNING— A VERY GOOD PLACE TO END

I began this chapter by going back to Paradise-—a world in harmony with itself, with human beings in intimate relationship with each other and God. But Paradise was lost. We now live in a world of conflict and pain. We are separated from each other and God and are caught in the cosmic struggle between good and evil. We are sinners in a fallen and broken world. But the good news is that what was lost—Paradise—can be regained because of the first and second comings of Jesus Christ.

Paradise regained: The first coming of Christ. Jesus came the first time as our substitute for sin. He accepted God's wrath against sin and offered himself as a sacrifice to pay the penalty for our sin. Through faith in Christ we can be forgiven and restored to the intimacy with God for which we were originally created. This relationship with God introduces us to a whole new way of living in relationship with one another. Instead of competition and control, we can be mutually submissive to each other (Ephesians 5:21) and love and care for each other (1 Corinthians 13). The brokenness of the Fall has been restored and healed through Christ.

Paradise regained: The Second Coming. While the first coming of Christ restores us to God and each other, his second coming brings justice to the earth and restores creation to a new and living way.

> Then I saw a new heaven and a new earth, for the first heaven and the first earth had passed away, and there was no longer any sea. . . .

"He will wipe every tear from their eyes. There will be no more death or mourning or crying or pain, for the old order of things has passed away."

He who was seated on the throne said, "I am making everything new!" Then he said, "Write this down, for these words are trustworthy and true."   *Revelation 21:1, 4–5*

Chapter 3

ISRAEL: GOD'S FOCUS FOR THE FUTURE

It was one of those meetings I will never forget. I was invited to join about twenty evangelical leaders and politicians at the Blair House in Washington, D.C., to meet with Menachem Begin, the prime minister of Israel. It was a rather distinguished group of people, among them U.S. Sen. John Warner, journalist Cal Thomas, seminary president John F. Walvoord, and evangelist Grady Wilson. We were ushered into a room with the appropriate number of chairs. We sat in two rows in a semicircle with three chairs facing us.

After a considerable wait, the prime minister entered the room with the Israeli ambassador to the United States and the Rev. Jerry Falwell, who had arranged this private meeting. The three of them sat facing us. The prime minister spoke for a while about the political and security issues facing Israel. He spoke in a quiet voice, and everyone leaned forward to catch everything he said.

When Mr. Begin finished, Jerry Falwell asked if we would each respond with a brief statement. This had not been mentioned before the meeting, and I was not prepared to say anything. I knew I was not an "evangelical leader," as many of the others in the room were. I had been invited to this meeting because I worked for Jerry Falwell. I was there on his merit, not my own. As others spoke to the prime minister, my mind was racing trying to figure out what to say. I didn't want to sound stupid! Finally it was my turn.

"Mr. Prime Minister," I began. "I am by far the youngest member of this distinguished group of American leaders. I am part of the next generation. As a member of this generation, I want to assure you of our support for the State of Israel. Be assured that the protection of Israel will be guaranteed in my generation and—with God's help—the next generation also."

I remember the prime minister's smiling when I finished, but I was feeling so relieved that I do not remember what he said. I learned later that he was deeply moved by my words because of his concern for the security and future of Israel. As we left the Blair House and walked down the street, we were hounded by journalists taking photographs and asking questions about our meeting. For a brief moment, I felt I was a little part of history—both biblical history and modern history. The existence of the State of Israel brings together biblical prophecy and modern history as has not been seen since the days of the New Testament. The regathering of the Jews to Israel and their existence as a nation is the *most significant* prophetic event since Jesus ascended to heaven.

THE FINAL QUESTION

> "Lord, are you at this time going to restore the kingdom to Israel?"   *Acts 1:6*

Jesus had been with his disciples for three years of public and private ministry. They had heard the Sermon on the Mount and the Olivet Discourse. They had seen Peter walk on water and had assisted in feeding more than five thousand people with five loaves and two fish. They had been with Jesus during his triumphal entry into Jerusalem and during the moving supper in the Upper Room. They had been through the despair of the Cross and the glorious surprise of the Resurrection. They had spent time with Jesus after that. During all their journey together they had intimate access to their leader. They watched and listened to him. They asked questions of him. Now Jesus was about to leave. All they had seen, heard, and done was now reduced to one final question: "Lord, are you at this time going to restore the kingdom to Israel?"

This final question raises two significant prophetic issues: the restoration of the kingdom to Israel, and the role of Jesus in restoring the kingdom. Not all Bible scholars agree that there is a future kingdom for Israel. Some believe that the Old Testament promises of that kingdom are allegorical in nature and are already fulfilled in a spiritual sense in the church. That is, the church is "Israel" in the New Testament. But the clear meaning of the disciples' final question contradicts that interpretation. They were looking for a real kingdom—Israel—restored by a real person—Jesus.

Note that Jesus did not correct the disciples' understanding of a future kingdom for Israel. He did not say, "There will be no future kingdom for Israel. My program for Israel is over. All that I promised to Israel is fulfilled in the church." Instead, Jesus confirmed his belief in the future kingdom and simply said, "It is not for you to know the times or dates the Father has set by his own authority" (Acts 1:7). The time and date of the future kingdom has been set; it will come by the authority and power of the Father.

DOES GOD HAVE A FUTURE PLAN FOR ISRAEL?

That final question asked of Jesus reveals the disciples' hope of a restoration of the kingdom to Israel. And their hope was not an isolated idea. Rather, it is central to the teaching of both the Old and New Testaments.

The Future Kingdom and Old Testament Prophecy

The inquiry of the disciples was a biblically informed question. It was shaped by their understanding of various Old Testament prophecies. Isaiah had predicted this future kingdom as a messianic age when many people will go to Jerusalem to worship at the temple and God's law will go out from Zion (Isaiah 2:1–3). In "the last days" God will settle international disputes and people will "beat their swords into plowshares and their spears into pruning hooks" (v. 4). War will cease, and people will "walk in the light of the LORD" (vv. 4–5).

Messiah is identified as "Wonderful Counselor, Mighty God, Everlasting Father, Prince of Peace" (Isaiah 9:6). It is predicted that he will "reign on David's throne and over his kingdom, establishing and upholding it with justice and righteousness from that time on and forever" (v. 7). When the "shoot" grows from the "stump of Jesse" (Isaiah 11:1), then "the wolf will live with the lamb" and the previous hostilities in creation will be resolved (vv. 6, 9).

The coming of Messiah to establish this kingdom on the earth will also include a regathering of the Jewish people to the land of Israel. God will bring them from the east, the west, the north, and the south—"from the ends of the earth" (Isaiah 43:5–6).

These predictions from the book of Isaiah are part of a larger body of prophetic material in the Old Testament that predicts a scattering of the Jewish people throughout the world, their regathering to Israel, and the coming of Messiah to sit on David's throne and rule the entire world. All these prophecies are about a real throne (David's), a real king (Messiah), and a real kingdom (Israel).

The Future Kingdom and the Virgin Mary

In chapter 2 we compared the two advents of Jesus Christ. During the first advent he came to suffer, die, and rise again for our redemption. During his second advent he will come to earth to establish his kingdom as predicted in the Old Testament Scriptures.

In coming the first time, Jesus was born of the Virgin Mary. God sent an angel to announce to Mary that she would be mother of "the Son of the Most High." "You have found favor with God," the angel said. "You will be with child and give birth to a son, and you are to give him the name Jesus" (Luke 1:30–31). But the message of the angel does not stop there. "He will be great," the angel continued. "The Lord God will give him the throne of his father David, and he will reign over the house of Jacob forever; his kingdom will never end" (vv. 32–33). The first part of the prophecy has already been fulfilled: Jesus was born of Mary. The second part still awaits fulfillment: He will reign forever on the throne of David.

The Future Kingdom and the Teaching of Paul

Nowhere in the entire New Testament is the future of Israel as a nation and a people more clearly explained than in chapters 9–11 of the book of Romans. First, Paul stated that the Jews have a special relationship to God. "Theirs is the adoption as sons; theirs the divine glory, the covenants, the receiving of the law, the temple worship and the promises" (Romans 9:4). Second, Israel has experienced "a hardening." The Jews have become resistant to the gospel, and as a result, the gospel has been offered to the Gentiles (11:25). Third, God has *not* rejected Israel. "Did God reject his people?" Paul asks. "By no means!" he answers. "God did not reject his people." (vv. 1–2). Fourth, when God has called the "full number of the Gentiles," he will then restore the kingdom to Israel and "all Israel will be saved" (vv. 25–26).

Does God have a future plan for Israel? Absolutely! All his promises toward Israel will be fulfilled. To doubt this future hope is to ignore the clear teaching of both the Old and New Testaments. In the last days God will bring this future kingdom into existence and Jesus Christ will rule in Israel and over all the earth. Jesus reminded his disciples that the times and dates for these events are already set (Acts 1:7).

THE JEWS: A HISTORY OF SUFFERING
AND REDEMPTION

No people group on the face of the earth is more resilient
than the Jews. Their existence as a people today is a testimony to
their incredible journey against all odds. No people have been
more persecuted, harassed, or hated. Their history is replete with
the Pharaohs, Hamans, and Hitlers of the world. Yet they have survived. In his monumental work *A History of the Jews*, Paul Johnson calls them the "most tenacious people in history" and points
to the city of Hebron as living proof of their tenacity.[1] He describes
the many peoples who conquered and controlled this city—many
of whom drove out the Jews or attacked them or murdered them.
Johnson writes:

> So when the historian visits Hebron today, he asks himself:
> Where are all the peoples which once held this place? Where
> are the Canaanites? Where are the Edomites? Where are the
> ancient Hellenes and the Romans, the Byzantines, the
> Franks, the Mamluks and the Ottomans? They have vanished
> into time, irrevocably. But the Jews are still in Hebron.[2]

The history of the Jews is one of repeated cycles of suffering followed by redemption. These cycles are as old as the suffering under the cruel hand of the Pharaoh in Egypt with the
redemption through the Exodus under Moses. They are as modern as the Holocaust and the resultant establishment of the State
of Israel. In between these events lie nearly six thousand years
of similar history.

In this cycle of suffering and redemption, two events seem
to shape the thinking of modern Jewry: the Holocaust and the formation of the State of Israel. They are connected events. Johnson writes that the Holocaust was "a prime causative factor in the
creation of the state of Israel. . . . The creation of Israel was the
consequence of Jewish suffering."[3] Both events are crucial to
understanding the future of Israel.

The Holocaust: The Depths of Anti-Semitism

Several years ago I attended a conference sponsored by the Anti-Defamation League of B'nai B'rith. On the flight home, I began to read a book I had received at the conference, *Auschwitz: Beginning of a New Era? Reflections of the Holocaust.* As I read the heart-wrenching testimonies of the deepest human sufferings, it was as if I were transported back in time to an era we would prefer to forget. It was a painful exercise, and I fought the overwhelming urge to break down and sob. I kept asking the question, "Was I to blame?" even though I was not even living during the Nazi nightmare. I pondered, "What would I have done had I been there? Would I have resisted and been willing to die with the Jewish community, or would I, like so many Protestants and Catholics, have justified my silence on the grounds that the Holocaust was not really my problem?" These are questions we must all face as we look back on this abyss of human depravity.

The Holocaust, which occurred between 1933 and 1945, was a conscious attempt by the Nazi regime to eradicate all the Jews of Europe. The statistics of this genocide are so staggering that they are difficult to comprehend. A total of 6 million Jews were murdered, including more than 80 percent of the intellectual and cultural leaders of the community. In 1944, under the threat of the advancing Allied armies, the rate of extermination was increased so that 10,000 Hungarian Jews were killed every day. There loomed the possibility that no Jews at all would survive. Perhaps the best way to understand this tragedy is to hear the words of some Jews who lived through it. This is the testimony of a Polish guard at the Auschwitz extermination camp, as given at the Nuremburg war trials that followed World War II.

> Witness: Women carrying children were (always) sent with them in the crematorium. (Children were of no labor value so they were killed. The mothers were sent along, too, because separation might lead to panic, hysteria—which might slow up the destruction process, and this could not be

afforded. It was simpler to condemn the mothers too and keep things quiet and smooth.) The children were then torn from their parents outside the crematorium and sent to the gas chambers separately. (At that point, crowding more people into the gas chambers became the most urgent consideration. Separating meant that more children could be packed in separately, or they could be thrown in over the heads of adults once the chamber was packed.) When the extermination of the Jews in the gas chambers was at its height, orders were issued that children were to be thrown straight into the crematorium furnaces, or into a pit near the crematorium, without being gassed first.

Smirnov (Russian prosecutor): How am I to understand this? Did they throw them into the fire alive, or did they kill them first?

Witness: They threw them in alive. Their screams could be heard at the camp. It is difficult to say how many children were destroyed in this way.

Smirnov: Why did they do this?

Witness: It's very difficult to say. We don't know whether they wanted to economize on gas, or if it was because there was not enough room in the gas chambers.[4]

These descriptions defy comment. But we must hear the screams of the children, smell the stench of death, feel the pain of suffering, and never forget! As Christians we cannot turn our backs on this chapter of history. To dismiss it as someone else's problem is to sow seeds of apathy that would permit the genocide to occur again. To justify it with the claim that the Jews deserved it because they crucified Jesus is abhorrent.

The Holocaust is central to the thinking of every Jew in the world. The Holocaust is a reminder of the intense hatred toward Jews that has existed throughout history. Although the Holocaust is past, anti-Semitism remains. The Jews now have their own nation and possess the third most powerful military force in the world. But they are not safe. They are surrounded by hostile neighbors bent on their total extinction. It is this kind of hostility, so palpable during the Holocaust, that will set the stage for the final battle—Armageddon.

The Birth of Modern Israel

When I met Menachem Begin at the Blair House, he seemed like a kindly grandfather. His gentle demeanor defied his history as a resistance leader who through acts of terrorism broke the will of the British in Palestine and paved the way for the establishment of the Jewish State. Begin was from Brest-Litovsk in Poland. Before the war there were more than thirty thousand Jews in that city; by 1944, only ten were left. Begin was arrested by the Soviets during the war and sent to a prison near the Arctic Circle. Upon release from prison, he walked through Asia to Palestine and founded Irgun—a resistance movement.[5] Irgun was responsible for blowing up various government buildings. On July 22, 1946, Begin was responsible for a bomb at the King David Hotel that killed Britons, Arabs, and Jews.

The next year, the United Nations voted to partition Palestine into two states—Jewish and Arab. On May 14, 1948, the State of Israel was officially established. David Ben-Gurion, who became the nation's first prime minister, read the Scroll of Independence in the Tel Aviv Museum: "By virtue of our national and intrinsic right and on the strength of the resolution of the United Nations General Assembly, we hereby declare the establishment of a Jewish State in Palestine, which shall be known as the State of Israel."[6] The Arab response was to declare war on Israel, but the nation survived. Israel expanded its territory during the Six-Day War in 1967. Initially, half of Jerusalem was under Arab control and half under Jewish control. After the Six-Day War, Jerusalem came under exclusive Jewish control and remains that way today.

THE REGATHERING OF ISRAEL TO THE LAND

Israel now exists as a nation among the nations. For the first time since the first century A.D., the Jews possess the land of

Palestine. They existed for more than 1,900 years in villages and cities all over the world. They endured persecution, harassment, imprisonment, and death. They wandered the earth as nomads— no place to call their own. But all that has changed. From these same far-flung villages and cities they have returned to the land— person by person, family by family. Their presence in the land today is nothing short of a modern-day miracle. It is a miracle clearly predicted in the Bible and closely associated with the coming of Jesus Christ and the end of the world.

Predictions in the Bible

> In that day the Lord will reach out his hand a second time to reclaim the remnant that is left of his people from Assyria, from Lower Egypt, from Upper Egypt, from Cush, from Elam, from Babylonia, from Hamath and from the islands of the sea.

> *He will raise a banner for the nations*
> *and gather the exiles of Israel;*
> *he will assemble the scattered people of Judah*
> *from the four quarters of the earth.*
> *Isaiah 11:11–12*

In this chapter the prophet is describing the future millennial kingdom. He begins by declaring that a descendant of David (v. 1) will judge the entire earth (v. 4). It will be a time of peace and harmony. The "wolf will live with the lamb" (v. 6), and "the cow will feed with the bear" (v. 7). The entire earth "will be full of the knowledge of the LORD" (v. 9). All these prophecies still await fulfillment.

In conjunction with these predictions, the prophet also foretold the regathering of the Jewish people to the land. They would be gathered "from the four quarters of the earth" (v. 12). Note that this regathering was not to be the first such event, but rather, the "second time." We already know about the first regathering. After seventy years in exile, the Jews returned to the land under the leadership of Zerubbabel, Ezra, and Nehemiah. They rebuilt Jerusalem and the city walls. Isaiah predicted these events and declared that they would be connected to the ultimate hope of Messiah's coming to sit on David's throne to rule the world. Until 1949, this prospect was an impossibility—but no longer.

Two Stages: Physical and Spiritual

> Then he said to me: "Son of man, these bones are the whole house of Israel. They say, 'Our bones are dried up and our hope is gone; we are cut off.' Therefore prophesy and say to them: 'This is what the Sovereign LORD says: O my people, I am going to open your graves and bring you up from them; I will bring you back to the land of Israel. Then you, my people, will know that I am the LORD, when I open your graves and bring you up from them. I will put my Spirit in you and you will live, and I will settle you in your own land. Then you will know that I the LORD have spoken, and I have done it, declares the LORD.' "   *Ezekiel 37:11–14*

These verses are from the account of Ezekiel's vision of a valley of dry bones. God shows Ezekiel the valley and asks the question, "Son of Man, can these bones live?" (v. 2). Ezekiel is then told to prophesy and speak to the bones so that they will live. As he preaches, the bones come to life in two stages. First, there is a "rattling sound" (v. 7). The bones join together and take on tendons, flesh, and skin, but they are not breathing. Second, "breath entered them; they came to life and stood up on their feet—a vast army" (v. 10).

The bones represent the "whole house of Israel" (v. 11). As they lie in the valley, they represent the nation of Israel scattered throughout the world. They are without hope and "cut off" from the land. But God will one day change their condition. The change will occur in two stages. First, the Jews will be regathered physically to the land. God promises, "I will bring you back to the land of Israel" (v. 12). This is symbolized by the coming together of the bones and their receiving tendons, flesh, and skin. Second, when the Jews return to the land they will experience a spiritual rebirth.

God says, "I will put my Spirit in you and you will live, and I will settle you in your own land" (v. 14).

Today Israel is living between these two stages. They have been regathered to the land, but they live there in unbelief. One day, when Jesus returns, all Israel will be saved (Romans 9:25–27). In preparation for that day, Israel will first of all go through a time of great tribulation and distress. Hostility toward the Jews will increase. A major coalition of armies will declare war against them. They will come again to the very brink of extinction. But then Jesus will come and defeat these armies at the Battle of Armageddon and establish his kingdom in Israel. In that day God will "give them an undivided heart and put a new spirit in them; I will remove from them their heart of stone and give them a heart of flesh. . . . They will be my people, and I will be their God" (Ezekiel 11:19–20).

The Necessity of the Regathering

All the events that surround the coming of Jesus to the earth and the end of the world require that Israel exist as a nation in the land of Palestine. In future chapters we will discuss these events in detail, including the following:

1. A time of tribulation
2. A peace treaty with Israel
3. Arab-Jewish hostility
4. The rebuilding of the temple
5. The Battle of Armageddon
6. The coming of Jesus to reign on David's throne
7. The establishment of Christ's kingdom from Jerusalem

None of these events is possible if the Jews are dispersed among the nations without a homeland. The geopolitical situation during the end times requires the existence of Israel as a nation. The return of Israel to the land is the *most significant* prophetic event since the first century.

Some biblical scholars believe that the rebirth of Israel in 1949 signals the beginning of the terminal generation—the generation that will live to see the coming of Jesus. This is based on the words of Jesus in the Olivet Discourse (Matthew 24–25). In this discourse Jesus deals with the "signs" that will accompany his second coming to the earth. He talks about wars, famines, and earthquakes (24:6–7); about persecution of Christians (v. 9); about false Christs and the preaching of the gospel to the whole world (vv. 11–13); about the abomination of desolation in the temple (vv. 15–16); and about distress in Palestine (vv. 20–22).

Jesus tells the disciples to watch the fig tree. When the leaves come out, summer is near—that is, when we see these events begin to occur, we will know the end is near. Some scholars believe that the fig tree represents the regathering of Israel. Whether or not this is so, it is clear from the teaching of Jesus that Israel will inhabit the land prior to his second coming. Then Jesus says this:

> "I tell you the truth, this generation will certainly not pass away until all these things have happened." *Matthew 24:34*

If the fig tree represents Israel and its regathering to the land, then the generation that sees it happen will "not pass away until all these things have happened." Consequently, some mark 1949 as the beginning of the last generation to live before Jesus returns. While this is certainly a possible interpretation of this text, it is by no means the only one. Some believe that this prediction was fulfilled in the lives of the apostles who lived to see the destruction of Jerusalem in A.D. 70. Others believe it refers to the survival of the Jewish people (that is, the word *generation* is taken to refer to race). In this view, the Jews will not pass into extinction, but will live to see these things fulfilled.

Whatever the correct interpretation, one thing is abundantly clear—Israel is back in the land, and this is one of the major events that signals the end of the world. The Jews have been gathered a second time. They will endure a time of suffering (the Tribulation) that will once again lead to their redemption (the return of Messiah to establish the kingdom). What was thought as impossible little more than a half-century ago is now a reality. How long they will be in the land before Jesus comes, we do not know. But we

know that before he comes, they are to have possession of the
land—and they do! In light of this fact, the words of Jesus ought
to take on new meaning.

> "When these things begin to take place, stand up and lift
> up your heads, because your redemption is drawing near."
>
> *Luke 21:28*

Chapter 4

THE END OF THE WORLD ACCORDING TO DANIEL

Although Israel will be the focus of attention toward the end of the world, God also has a specific program for the rest of the nations of the world. His plan for the non-Jewish nations is outlined very clearly in the prophetic Scriptures. The prophet Daniel gives the most concise overview of the geopolitical situation that will exist prior to the second coming of Jesus Christ. Nearly all students of prophecy agree that the prophecies of Daniel are the most important in the entire Old Testament that deal with end times. They are also some of the most difficult to discern and understand.

Whenever I think of these complex prophecies, I remember what happened on Thanksgiving Day several years ago. My mother and father had joined us for the midday feast, and afterward I invited Dad to play golf. He said, "You know, I've always wanted to play golf. I have never played golf in my life, so I would love to go." I got him a pair of sneakers and lent him my son's set of clubs.

I will never forget the first hole we played. I put the ball down, chose a three wood, and whacked the ball—and it went to the far side of the next fairway over. My dad got up and adjusted his cap. I told him how to hold the club. He set the ball, took a swing, and hit the top of the ball. It rolled three or four feet. I said, "Dad, don't worry about it. It's a tough sport. Take another ball and try again." So he set a second ball. Adjusted his cap. Took a swing and missed the ball completely! He looked at me with that twinkle in his eye and said, "This is a really difficult course."[1]

That is how I feel about the prophetic section of the book of Daniel. It is a pretty tough course—lots of hazards, sand traps, woods, narrow fairways, and difficult greens. But I am going to take a swing, and I hope I am reasonably on target.[2]

A DAZZLING STATUE

King Nebuchadnezzar of Babylon had a troubling and disturbing dream (see Daniel 2:24–49). He called in his wise men and put them to the test. "Okay, you're wise—then you must do two things," he said. "Number one, you must tell me what my dream is; I'm not going to tell you—you must tell me. Then, number two, after you have told me my dream, you must give the interpretation."

This lay beyond the abilities of the wise men. They responded, "King Nebuchadnezzar, no king however great or mighty has ever made such a request. This is impossible!" Nebuchadnezzar replied, "Impossible or not, you must do it, or I will cut you into pieces." They could not do it, so their execution was set.

Daniel was one of the wise men, but he apparently was not present when the king issued his ultimatum. The king's guards arrived to kill Daniel, who asked, "Why was the decree issued?" The story was explained to Daniel. He gathered his friends together for a prayer meeting, and God answered his prayer. God revealed the dream and the interpretation. Daniel then went to the king both to reveal and to interpret the dream.

"There Is a God in Heaven"

> Daniel replied, "No wise man, enchanter, magician or diviner can explain to the king the mystery he has asked about, but there is a God in heaven who reveals mysteries. He has shown King Nebuchadnezzar what will happen in days to come. Your dream and the visions that passed through your mind as you lay on your bed are these:. . ."
>
> *Daniel 2:27–28*

The wise men had admitted that they could not tell him the dream. Moreover, they said the problem lay even beyond the ability of their gods to solve. "What the king asks is too difficult. No one can reveal it to the king except the gods, and they do not live among men" (v. 11). But what the wise men and their gods could not do, Daniel and his God did. And Daniel placed the credit where it belonged: "But there is a God in heaven."

The Dream

> "You looked, O king, and there before you stood a large statue—an enormous, dazzling statue, awesome in appearance. The head of the statue was made of pure gold, its chest and arms of silver, its belly and thighs of bronze, its legs of iron, its feet partly of iron and partly of baked clay. While you were watching, a rock was cut out, but not by human hands. It struck the statue on its feet of iron and clay and smashed them. Then the iron, the clay, the bronze, the silver and the gold were broken to pieces at the same time and became like chaff on a threshing floor in the summer. The wind swept them away without leaving a trace. But the rock that struck the statue became a huge mountain and filled the whole earth."
>
> *Vv. 31–35*

As we consider the meaning of this dream, there are three important preliminary observations to keep in mind. First, from the head of the statue to the feet, the quality of the material deteriorates—gold, silver, bronze, iron, clay. Second, as the quality deteriorates, the strength increases. Third, the various parts of the statue represent world powers and their influence in human history.

1. *The head of gold*

"This was the dream, and now we will interpret it to the king. You, O king, are the king of kings. The God of heaven has given you dominion and power and might and glory; in your hands he has placed mankind and the beasts of the field and the birds of the air. Wherever they live, he has made you ruler over them all. You are that head of gold."

Vv. 36–38

The head of gold represents Nebuchadnezzar and the Babylonian Empire. The Babylonians were known for their love of gold. Nebuchadnezzar wanted to build Babylon as a city of gold. He ruled on a throne of gold. He built a statue of gold that stood ninety feet high and nine feet wide. Herodotus, who visited Babylon seventy years after Nebuchadnezzar's passing, noted that he had never seen such an abundance of gold as he saw there.

Every year, Babylon would celebrate the coming of the new year with a massive festival. Nebuchadnezzar and the kings who followed him would be ushered in to sit upon a throne of gold. The court would read the ancient epic of creation as it was written down by the Babylonians. They would honor Marduk, their creator-god. Then they would worship the king as the earthly representative of Marduk. They declared that the king ruled, not only peoples, but beasts and animals and birds and all of creation— words echoed by Daniel in his salutation to Nebuchadnezzar.

2. *The chest and arms of silver*

"After you, another kingdom will rise, inferior to yours."

V. 39

Very little is said in the text about the second empire, but nearly all Bible scholars agree that it refers to the Medo-Persian Empire, which replaced the Babylonian Empire. The word for silver in Aramaic is also the word for taxation. The Medo-Persians became known for their extensive system of taxation. All taxes were paid in silver (unlike the Babylonian Empire, where taxes were paid in gold). So the silver represents the second world power that would rise to domination.

3. *The stomach and thighs of brass*

> "Next, a third kingdom, one of bronze, will rule over the whole earth."   *V. 39*

The third kingdom was the Greek Empire. If we were living through some of these events, we would readily understand the significance of these prophetic details. A Medo-Persian soldier would be dressed in a cloth turban and a cloth upper tunic with full arms and trousers. But a Greek soldier would have a helmet of brass, a breastplate of brass, a shield of brass, and a sword of brass.

4. *Legs and feet of iron*

> "Finally, there will be a fourth kingdom, strong as iron— for iron breaks and smashes everything—and as iron breaks things to pieces, so it will crush and break all the others. Just as you saw that the feet and toes were partly of baked clay and partly of iron, so this will be a divided kingdom; yet it will have some of the strength of iron in it, even as you saw iron mixed with clay. As the toes were partly iron and partly clay, so this kingdom will be partly strong and partly brittle. And just as you saw the iron mixed with baked clay, so the people will be a mixture and will not remain united, any more than iron mixes with clay."   *Vv. 40–43*

The fourth kingdom represents the Roman Empire, and Daniel deals with it at greater length than the others. The iron describes the disciplined regimen of Roman soldiers who would conquer the known world. The statue describes several unique characteristics of the Roman Empire.

First, it appeared to have two dimensions. The legs were made of pure iron, but the toes and feet were made of baked clay and iron. Yet they were all part of one empire.

Second, the feet are unique. The feet were composed of a mixture of clay and iron, two elements that do not combine into one substance. This would imply a union in which the components maintain separate identities.

Third, this mixture may imply some sort of political or economic cooperation. At the same time, national and cultural identities would be maintained. It will be one empire, but it will be divided.

The Stone Crushes the Feet

> "In the time of those kings, the God of heaven will set up a kingdom that will never be destroyed, nor will it be left to another people. It will crush all those kingdoms and bring them to an end, but it will itself endure forever. This is the meaning of the vision of the rock cut out of a mountain, but not by human hands—a rock that broke the iron, the bronze, the clay, the silver and the gold to pieces." *Vv. 44–45*

So we see that in the course of human history there arose these four major world powers—Babylon, Medo-Persia, Greece, and Rome. But at some point God will intervene into history and crush all previous world powers. He will set up a kingdom of his own, after which there will be no other human kingdoms.

Christ is the Rock

What does the stone that smashes the statues represent? What is its significance? It is a stone cut without hands, and it becomes a mountain that encompasses the earth. Here we have to be careful not to speculate, but to allow the Scriptures to interpret themselves whenever possible. Two other Old Testament passages deal with a stone.

1. *The rejected stone*

> *The stone the builders rejected*
>   *has become the capstone;*
> *the LORD has done this,*
>   *and it is marvelous in our eyes.*
> > *Psalm 118:22–23*

Who is this stone? These verses are quoted twice in the New Testament, and both times the stone is identified as Jesus Christ. First, Jesus applies this prophecy to himself.

Jesus looked directly at them and asked, "Then what is the meaning of that which is written:

> " 'The stone the builders rejected
> has become the capstone'?"
>
> *Luke 20:17*

Second, Peter applies this verse to Jesus in an address before the Sanhedrin.

"Then know this, you and all the people of Israel: It is by the name of Jesus Christ of Nazareth, whom you crucified but whom God raised from the dead, that this man stands before you healed. He is

> " 'the stone you builders rejected,
> which has become the capstone.' "
>
> *Acts 4:10*

2. The cornerstone

So this is what the Sovereign LORD says:

> "See, I lay a stone in Zion,
>   a tested stone,
> a precious cornerstone for a sure foundation;
>   the one who trusts will never be dismayed."
>
> *Isaiah 28:16*

The significance of this second Old Testament reference to a stone is, like the first, revealed in the New Testament. The stone refers to Jesus Christ. Paul states this in Romans 9:33, and Peter says the same thing in 1 Peter 2:6–7.

For in Scripture it says:

> "See, I lay a stone in Zion,
>   a chosen and precious cornerstone,
> and the one who trusts in him
>   will never be put to shame."

Now to you who believe, this stone is precious. But to those who do not believe,

> "The stone the builders rejected
> has become the capstone."

It is safe to conclude that the stone mentioned in Daniel refers to Jesus Christ because the other two prophetic statements about a stone in the Old Testament refer to him.

So what is the meaning of the stone for Nebuchadnezzar's dream? Conservative scholars agree that the stone represents the rise and fall of human empires. It represents the coming of Jesus Christ, the living stone, to set up his kingdom on the earth. In the dream, Christ's coming is connected to the Roman Empire.

The legs of iron and the feet of clay and iron may represent two stages of influence for the Roman Empire. The first is a time of purity and strength; the second, a renewed coalition of people, nations, and people groups loosely formed into a political coalition similar to the Roman Empire as it existed centuries ago. So we can say that well over two thousand years ago, God predicted the rise and fall of major world empires and the eventual coming of Jesus at the end of the world to set up his kingdom.

THE FOUR BEASTS

Another prophetic passage concerns Daniel's vision of the four beasts (see Daniel 7:1–28).

In the first year that Belshazzar, Nebuchadnezzar's grandson, was king of Babylon, Daniel had a vision as he was lying on his bed.

> "In my vision at night I looked, and there before me were the four winds of heaven churning up the great sea. Four great beasts, each different from the others, came up out of the sea."   *Vv. 2–3*

The wind and the sea have symbolic significance elsewhere in Scripture.

1. *The wind.* Throughout the Bible, wind is symbolic of the power and sovereignty of God. It often represents God's working in the events of human history.

> But God remembered Noah and all the wild animals and the livestock that were with him in the ark, and he sent a wind over the earth, and the waters receded.   *Genesis 8:1*

God protected Noah, his family, and the animals from the great Flood while the rest of the world was destroyed. God then caused a wind to blow so that the waters of the Flood would recede. This wind represents the movement of God.

> So Moses stretched out his staff over Egypt, and the LORD made an east wind blow across the land all that day and all that night. By morning the wind had brought the locusts. . . .
> Moses then left Pharaoh and prayed to the LORD. And the LORD changed the wind to a very strong west wind, which caught up the locusts and carried them into the Red Sea. Not a locust was left anywhere in Egypt.
>
> *Exodus 10:13, 18–19*

God used the wind to accomplish a specific purpose. It was a tangible demonstration of his power and sovereignty in the events of people and nations.

2. *The sea.* The second symbol in this vision often represents humanity in the pages of the Bible.

> *Oh, the raging of many nations—*
>   *they rage like the raging sea!*
> *Oh, the uproar of the peoples—*
>   *they roar like the roaring of great waters!*
> *Although the peoples roar like the roar of surging waters,*
>   *when he rebukes them they flee far away,*
> *driven before the wind like chaff on the hills,*
>   *like tumbleweed before a gale.*
>
> *Isaiah 17:12–13*

Notice that both symbols are used in these verses. The nations are represented by the sea, and God's activity is represented by the wind.

3. *The four beasts.* The beasts in Daniel's vision represent the rise of four different world empires. When we put all these symbols together, we get a preliminary understanding of Daniel's dream: God moves (the wind) in the events of humanity (the sea) to give rise to four separate kingdoms (four beasts).

L B L B

The four beasts, which represent four kingdoms, are identified as a lion, a bear, a leopard, and another that did not resemble any creature Daniel could name.

1. *The lion* (Babylonian Empire)

> "The first was like a lion, and it had the wings of an eagle. I watched until its wings were torn off and it was lifted from the ground so that it stood on two feet like a man, and the heart of a man was given to it."   *V. 4*

2. *The bear* (Medo-Persian Empire)

> "And there before me was a second beast, which looked like a bear. It was raised up on one of its sides, and it had three ribs in its mouth between its teeth. It was told, 'Get up and eat your fill of flesh!'"   *V. 5*

3. *The leopard* (Greek Empire)

> "After that, I looked, and there before me was another beast, one that looked like a leopard. And on its back it had four wings like those of a bird. This beast had four heads, and it was given authority to rule."   *V. 6*

4. *The unnamed beast* (Roman Empire)

> "After that, in my vision at night I looked, and there before me was a fourth beast—terrifying and frightening and very powerful. It had large iron teeth; it crushed and devoured its victims and trampled underfoot whatever was left. It was different from all the former beasts, and it had ten horns."   *Vv. 7–8*

The descriptions of these kingdoms are similar to the descriptions from Nebuchadnezzar's dream recounted in Daniel 2. In both these overviews of human history, the greatest attention is given to the last empire—the Roman Empire.

The Fourth Kingdom

The extensive details given about the fourth beast are not easy to understand or interpret.

"Then I wanted to know the true meaning of the fourth beast, which was different from all the others and most terrifying, with its iron teeth and bronze claws—the beast that crushed and devoured its victims and trampled underfoot whatever was left. I also wanted to know about the ten horns on its head and about the other horn that came up, before which three of them fell—the horn that looked more imposing than the others and that had eyes and a mouth that spoke boastfully. As I watched, this horn was waging war against the saints and defeating them, until the Ancient of Days came and pronounced judgment in favor of the saints of the Most High, and the time came when they possessed the kingdom."

Daniel 7:19–22

This is strange language. Here is an unusual animal that initially seizes power over the entire world. Out of this animal ten horns emerge. Then an eleventh horn comes along, and three of the ten horns give allegiance to it. It also opposes the saints and persecutes them. Then the Ancient of Days pronounces judgment in favor of the saints. What does all this mean? The explanation, as given to Daniel, can be best understood in a series of stages (vv. 23–27).

Stage 1

"He gave me this explanation: 'The fourth beast is a fourth kingdom that will appear on earth. It will be different from all the other kingdoms and will devour the whole earth, trampling it down and crushing it.'"   *V. 23*

This is the opening stage of the Roman Empire. After the Babylonian, Medo-Persian, and Greek empires have collapsed one by one, there will come another world power. This power will expand over the known civilized world until all is under its control.

Stage 2

"'The ten horns are ten kings who will come from this kingdom.'"   *V. 24*

There is apparently an initial phase of world domination by
the Roman Empire. These ten horns, representing ten kings, are
very likely a second phase of the empire. The Bible does not state
when this occurs—immediately after the ascendancy of the
empire, or a considerable time later—only that there will be two
stages of domination. The second phase will entail a coalition,
involving a political or economic alignment of states or countries.
There will be ten in number, and they will fall within the boundaries of the original Roman Empire.

Stage 3

> "'After them another king will arise, different from the
> earlier ones; he will subdue three kings. He will speak
> against the Most High and oppress his saints and try to
> change the set times and the laws. The saints will be handed
> over to him for a time, times and half a time.'"   *Vv. 24–25*

This king is represented by the eleventh horn, and on the
basis of Daniel's description, I believe this is a reference to the rise
of the Antichrist.

1. *"He will speak against the Most High."* The underlying
idea in this statement is that this person will attempt to elevate himself to the status of the Most High God. He not only will oppose
God, but will also seek to become God. This is precisely what the
New Testament predicts about the coming Antichrist.

> Don't let anyone deceive you in any way, for that day will
> not come until the rebellion occurs and the man of lawlessness
> is revealed, the man doomed to destruction. He will oppose
> and will exalt himself over everything that is called God or is
> worshiped, so that he sets himself up in God's temple, pro-
> claiming himself to be God.   *2 Thessalonians 2:3–4*

2. *He will oppress God's saints.* The verb used in this phrase
means "to wear out." It means to hassle, persecute, or oppose.

3. *He will "try to change the set times and the laws."* This
statement very likely refers to the changing of natural, civil, and
moral laws. It is interesting to note that the New Testament calls
the Antichrist a "man of lawlessness" (2 Thessalonians 2:3).

4. *"The saints will be handed over to him."* This persecution will last for "a time, times and half a time" (v. 25). How long will this be? The same phrase is used in Daniel 12:7 and explained later on in verse 11: "There will be 1,290 days." This "times" seems to be three and one-half years. Many interpreters believe that "time" equals one year. "Times" equals two or more years. Accepting "times" as two years, "time, times and half a times" would be three and one-half years.

Let us review for just a moment. Daniel says, "I want to know more about this last world empire." Here is the scenario:

With power, force, and might Rome will conquer the world. Out of that empire will emerge a political coalition of ten separate kingdoms. When that occurs, an eleventh king will come along who will forge an alliance with three countries, from which he will ultimately bring about world domination. When he attains world domination, the king will do several things. First, he will proclaim himself to be a god. Second, he will harass the saints. Third, he will attempt to change the laws. Fourth, the people of Israel will be delivered over to him to be harassed and persecuted for a specific period of time—namely, three and a half years.

If all of this sounds bleak, that's because it is. The good news is still to come.

THE COMING OF GOD

> "'But the court will sit, and his power will be taken away and completely destroyed forever. Then the sovereignty, power and greatness of the kingdoms under the whole heaven will be handed over to the saints, the people of the Most High. His kingdom will be an everlasting kingdom, and all rulers will worship and obey him.'"   *Daniel 7:26–27*

These verses describe how God will come in judgment to strip the beast of his power and establish his own kingdom and authority. Several characteristics of God's coming are worth noting.

1. *God will come in judgment.* The text describes it this way: "The court will sit."

2. *He will come to set up his kingdom.* God, not someone
   else, will set up his kingdom.
3. *His coming will be dramatic.* His coming will be a
   momentous intervention in human history.
4. *He will come in victory and triumph.* God's saints will
   govern a kingdom that will command obeisance from all
   earthly rulers and will last forever.

THE SEVENTY WEEKS

Still another prophetic passage in the book of Daniel deals
with the "seventy weeks." Many Bible scholars agree that Daniel
9:24–27 contains some of the most significant prophetic verses
in the entire Scriptures. I would add that they are also some of the
most difficult and confusing. How we interpret these verses deter-
mines our understanding of the events at the end of the world, the
time and manner of Jesus' second coming, the role of Israel in
future events, and finally, the relationship between Israel and the
Christian church—whether the latter is the spiritual extension of
the former, or whether they are separate institutions in the economy of God.

The Decree of Jewish History

"Seventy 'sevens' are decreed for your people and your
holy city to finish transgression, to put an end to sin, to atone
for wickedness, to bring in everlasting righteousness, to seal
up vision and prophecy and to anoint the most holy." *V. 24*

The opening verse of the prophecy identifies a decree about
Jewish history. Note three things about this decree:

1. *The length of time.* The Hebrew word translated "seven"
is a term used to designate a unit of time divided into seven segments. The unit could be hours, days, weeks, months, years—
whatever. The text refers to seventy units of time: "seventy 'sevens.'" Each unit is divided into seven segments. I believe that these
units refer to years. If this is the case, the text is referring to sev-

enty units of seven years, or 490 years. I believe this for two reasons. First, Daniel 9 begins with a reference to seventy years.

> In the first year of Darius son of Xerxes (a Mede by descent), who was made ruler over the Babylonian kingdom—in the first year of his reign, I, Daniel, understood from the Scriptures, according to the word of the LORD given to Jeremiah the prophet, that the desolation of Jerusalem would last seventy years.   *Vv. 1–2*

This is a literal statement, and it would make sense to carry this literal interpretation to the end of the chapter and conclude that the second "seventy" also refers to years. Second, the Jews were accustomed to the concept of a "week of years," or seven years. In earlier times they had observed the sabbatical year—the seventh year.

2. *The people involved.* The people included in this decree were "your people and your holy city" (v. 24). Daniel's people were the Jews; his holy city was Jerusalem. This situation represents a significant shift in the focus of the prophecies of Daniel. All his previous prophecies dealt with the Gentiles, not the Jews.

3. *The program of God.* Six things are listed that God is going to do during this period of 490 years. The first three were accomplished in the first advent of Christ, when he suffered, died, and rose again. The last three will be accomplished when Christ returns the second time. These six activities are as follows:

a. To finish transgression
b. To put an end to sin
c. To atone for wickedness
d. To bring in everlasting righteousness
e. To seal up the vision (that is, to close the pages on human history)
f. To anoint the most holy (to consecrate the temple)

God told the prophet, "I am going to reveal to you my program, which will include 490 years. That program has been cut out of human history. It is specifically for Israel and Jerusalem. During that period of time, these seventy weeks, six things will happen.

The first three deal with sin—and have already happened. The last three—ushering in everlasting righteousness, closing out human history, and consecrating the temple—remain to be fulfilled."

The Divisions of Jewish History

Three separate time periods are identified within the "seventy 'sevens'" in verses 25–27.

1. Seven "sevens" (v. 25) would be 7 x 7 years or 49 years.
2. Sixty-two "sevens" (v. 25) would be 62 x 7 years or 434 years.
3. One "seven" (v. 27) would be 1 x 7 years or 7 years.

So the 490-year span of time is divided into three periods: 49 years, 434 years, and 7 years. The text indicates that the first two time periods go together and deal with the rebuilding of Jerusalem and the first coming of Messiah.

Predictions About the Coming Messiah

"Know and understand this: From the issuing of the decree to restore and rebuild Jerusalem until the Anointed One, the ruler, comes, there will be seven 'sevens,' and sixty-two 'sevens.' It will be rebuilt with streets and a trench, but in times of trouble. After the sixty-two 'sevens,' the Anointed One will be cut off and will have nothing."   *Daniel 9:25–26*

The first prediction states that from the "issuing of the decree to restore and rebuild Jerusalem until the Anointed One" comes, there will be a total of 483 years (49 years and 434 years). To understand this prediction, we must identify the "decree." There were actually three decrees given to promote the rebuilding of Jerusalem as the Jews were returning to the land of Palestine from their exile in Babylon.

1. *The decree of Cyrus (538 B.C.)*

In the first year of Cyrus king of Persia, in order to fulfill the word of the LORD spoken by Jeremiah, the LORD moved the heart of Cyrus king of Persia to make a proclamation

throughout his realm and to put it in writing: "This is what
Cyrus king of Persia says: 'The LORD, the God of heaven, has
given me all the kingdoms of the earth and he has appointed
me to build a temple for him at Jerusalem in Judah. . . .' "

Ezra 1:1–2

This decree concerns the rebuilding of the temple. Although
the Jews actually rebuilt their houses and part of the city of
Jerusalem after this, the intent of the decree was focused on the
temple.

2. The decree of Artaxerxes (458 B.C.)

This is a copy of the letter King Artaxerxes had given to
Ezra the priest and teacher, a man learned in matters concerning the commands and decrees of the LORD for Israel:
". . . With this money be sure to buy bulls, rams and male
lambs, together with their grain offerings and drink offerings,
and sacrifice them on the altar of the temple of your God in
Jerusalem."

Ezra 7:11, 17

The second decree deals primarily with the restoration of
worship at the rebuilt temple.

3. The decree of Artaxerxes (445 B.C.)

The king said to me, "What is it you want?"
Then I prayed to the God of heaven, and I answered the
king, "If it pleases the king and if your servant has found
favor in his sight, let him send me to the city of Judah where
my fathers are buried so that I can rebuild it."
Then the king, with the queen sitting beside him, asked
me, "How long will your journey take, and when will you get
back?" It pleased the king to send me; so I set a time.

Nehemiah 2:4–6

The third decree deals exclusively with the rebuilding of the
city of Jerusalem—not the temple or its worship. This is most likely
the decree referred to in the prophecy of Daniel 9:25. The date of
the decree would therefore be 445 B.C. From this date until the Messiah comes will be 483 years. More precisely, there will be 483
years until Messiah is "cut off" and will have "nothing" (v. 26). This

is a reference to the death of the Anointed One and the fact that he does not establish an earthly kingdom. When we advance 483 years from 445 B.C., we arrive at the date A.D. 38.

This chronology poses a problem. Since Jesus died when he was thirty-three years old (A.D. 33), the dates are off by five years. However, this apparent discrepancy can be resolved. The Jewish calendar is different from the Gregorian calendar in common use today. The Jewish reckoning is built on lunar years of only 360 days; our calendar is structured on solar years of 365 days. When we calculate the difference between the calendars and factor that into the 69 weeks, we come up with the year A.D. 33. The prediction holds up to the exact year.

That takes care of the first two time periods. What do we make of the last "seven"—the final week?

The Last Week

> "The people of the ruler who will come will destroy the city and the sanctuary. The end will come like a flood: War will continue until the end, and desolations have been decreed. He will confirm a covenant with many for one 'seven.' In the middle of the 'seven' he will put an end to sacrifice and offering. And on a wing of the temple he will set up an abomination that causes desolation, until the end that is decreed is poured out on him."   *Daniel 9:26–27*

Who is the ruler? It is not Jesus Christ. He already came and was "cut off" (v. 26). The fact that these people will destroy the city (Jerusalem) and the sanctuary (the temple) means they are the enemies of God. Could the ruler therefore be the Antichrist? The rest of the prediction supports this idea. The Antichrist operates in this last seven-year span of time (v. 27). If these last seven years immediately followed the first 69 periods of time, it would mean the Antichrist would have been on the scene right after the death of Christ. But from our vantage point of history we know that this is not what happened. What, then, does this prediction mean? I suggest that between the sixty-ninth and seventieth weeks there is a parenthesis in human history. This is a period of time not dealt with in the prophecy. It is, in fact, the time period in which we are now living—the church age.

We may well ask, "If God knew about the church, why did he not put it into the prophecy as well?" This is a legitimate question. The answer lies in understanding that the concept of the church was a mystery throughout the Old Testament.

> For this reason I, Paul, the prisoner of Christ Jesus for the sake of you Gentiles—
>
> Surely you have heard about the administration of God's grace that was given to me for you, that is, the mystery made known to me by revelation, as I have already written briefly. In reading this, then, you will be able to understand my insight into the mystery of Christ, which was not made known to men in other generations as it has now been revealed by the Spirit to God's holy apostles and prophets. This mystery is that through the gospel the Gentiles are heirs together with Israel, members together of one body, and sharers together in the promise in Christ Jesus.   *Ephesians 3:1–6*

The mystery of the church was something that people before the apostle Paul's time did not understand. Daniel did not understand it, nor did the prophets Jeremiah and Isaiah. What was that mystery? That there would come a time in God's dealing with humanity when the distinction between Jew and Gentile would be irrelevant. God would extend his grace to everyone—Jews and Gentiles alike, male and female, bond and free. Together they would *all* be partakers of Jesus Christ. All would be one in Christ. It would have violated this mystery if God had clearly revealed it to Daniel in his incredible prophecy.

God in effect says to Daniel, "I am going to reveal to you my purpose for Israel and for Jerusalem. I am cutting out of history 490 years to deal with Israel and with Jerusalem. After the first sixty-nine weeks, Messiah will be crucified. Then, at the end of time I will return again to my people Israel in the seventieth week. Antichrist will come. Certain things will happen, and then I will return in glory."

"Okay, God," Daniel says. "What about in-between?"

God says, "Daniel, I can't tell you. It's a mystery. It's an unbelievable thing that I have in mind."

We can be thankful that we live in the parenthesis between the Crucifixion—the end of the sixty-ninth week—and the Second Coming, a parenthesis during which God's message of reconciliation is extended to all and not just one group of people.

The Tribulation Period

"He will confirm a covenant with many for one 'seven.'
In the middle of the 'seven' he will put an end to sacrifice and offering. And on a wing of the temple he will set up an abomination that causes desolation, until the end that is decreed is poured out on him."   *Daniel 9:27*

The Antichrist will do three things during the last seven years, which will be a troubled time known as the Tribulation.

1. He will confirm a covenant for seven years.
2. Halfway through, he will put an end to sacrifice and offering.
3. He will set up in the temple "an abomination that causes desolation."

The key phrases in understanding this prophecy are the "abomination that causes desolation" and the idea of three and a half years between the cessation of temple sacrifices and the introduction of the abomination. The prophecy implies that the Antichrist will forge a peace alliance with Israel for seven years. In the middle of that time period he will violate the agreement and put a stop to worship in the temple. Then he will desecrate the temple in the spirit of Antiochus Epiphanes, the Syrian king who reigned during the second century B.C. and became known for his desecration of the temple (see Daniel 8:25). This prophecy is repeated in Daniel 12:11, and the time period is indicated as 1,290 days, or three and a half years.

"From the time that the daily sacrifice is abolished and the abomination that causes desolation is set up, there will be 1,290 days."

The book of Revelation also speaks of this period of three and a half years in regard to the blasphemy by the Antichrist.

> The beast was given a mouth to utter proud words and blasphemies and to exercise his authority for forty-two months. He opened his mouth to blaspheme God, and to slander his name and his dwelling place and those who live in heaven. He was given power to make war against the saints and to conquer them. And he was given authority over every tribe, people, language and nation. All inhabitants of the earth will worship the beast—all whose names have not been written in the book of life belonging to the Lamb that was slain from the creation of the world.   *Revelation 13:5–8*

Jesus speaks of the abomination of desolation as one of the events that will precede his return to earth.

> "So when you see standing in the holy place 'the abomination that causes desolation,' spoken of through the prophet Daniel—let the reader understand—then let those who are in Judea flee to the mountains. Let no one on the roof of his house go down to take anything out of the house. Let no one in the field go back to get his cloak. How dreadful it will be in those days for pregnant women and nursing mothers! Pray that your flight will not take place in winter or on the Sabbath. For then there will be great distress, unequaled from the beginning of the world until now—and never to be equaled again."   *Matthew 24:15–21*

> "At that time the sign of the Son of Man will appear in the sky, and all the nations of the earth will mourn. They will see the Son of Man coming on the clouds of the sky, with power and great glory. And he will send his angels with a loud trumpet call, and they will gather his elect from the four winds, from one end of the heavens to the other."
> *Matthew 24:30–31*

All these prophecies refer to the last seven years prior to the coming of Christ. It will be a time of desolation and suffering. The temple will be devastated. The agreement made by the Antichrist will be broken. But Christ will come to defeat the Antichrist and his forces.

Where Is the Church?

In summary, the prophetic period of 490 years is divided into three parts. After 49 years—seven "weeks"—Jerusalem is rebuilt and the revelation to the Old Testament prophets is completed. At the sixty-ninth week—483 years into the total of 490—Messiah comes to earth, only to be crucified in the year A.D. 33. Then there occurs a parenthesis during which God extends his grace to people worldwide. At the end of time Messiah will return again to the nation of Israel and the city of Jerusalem. But just before he comes, the Antichrist will come onto the scene and form a coalition with Israel for seven years. In the middle of the seven years he will break that covenant. He will bring about the abomination of desolation and then *it* happens! God will close the envelope of history as we know it. He will seal the vision and say to the saints, "Folks, it's time to go back down." In glory, majesty, and power, Christ will return.

IS THE STAGE BEING SET?

The major focus of the prophecies of Daniel is the second stage of the Roman Empire. Daniel predicted that as we approach the end of the world and the coming of Jesus Christ, there will be a resurgent coalition of nations that were once part of that ancient empire. These nations will maintain individual identity, but form a political and economic partnership. Out of this partnership the Antichrist will rise to world domination.

In 1948, a number of European countries established the Organization for European Economic Co-operation (OEEC). This organization was in part a response to the horrors of World War II. These nations saw the need for global cooperation, a reduction of military force, renewed diplomacy, and less emphasis on national sovereignty.[3] This was the first step in an ongoing political journey toward the formation and development of the European Economic Community (EEC, or "Common Market") in 1958.

In 1951, six nations of Europe signed a treaty: France, Italy, West Germany, Belgium, The Netherlands, and Luxembourg. They clearly stated their objective:

> Resolved to substitute for historic rivalries a fusion of their essential interests: to establish, by creating an economic community, the foundation of a broad and independent community among people long divided by bloody conflicts; to lay the bases of institutions capable of ongoing direction to their future common destiny; have decided to create a European coal and steel community.[4]

The EEC continues to make progress toward these same goals. It has established four institutions to accomplish them.

1. *The High Authority.* A nine-member group given the responsibility to act in the best interests of the community as a whole
2. *Common Assembly.* Representatives from each country
3. *Council of Ministers.* Individual ministers from each member state
4. *Court of Justice.*

The EEC has remarkable parallels to the predictions of Daniel that relate to the final stages of the Roman Empire. With the fall of the Berlin Wall and the demise of communism in Eastern Europe in the late eighties, the concept of total European unity is now a realistic possibility. It appears to me that the ongoing political and economic unity of Europe is the fulfillment of Daniel's prophecies and the preparation for the coming of Antichrist.

Chapter 5

THE EMERGING NEW WORLD ORDER

It was December 1988. Eastern Europe was still under the control of communism. The Soviet Union was still a unified nation, with Mikhail Gorbachev in power. On December 7, Gorbachev gave a speech to the United Nations in which he introduced the idea of a "new world order." He said, "Further global progress is now possible only through a quest for universal consensus in the movement toward a new world order."[1] Since that occasion, the concept has gained worldwide acceptance. It reflects the current trend toward globalism—a trend that is clearly predicted in the Bible. As we approach the end of the world, there will be a dramatic shift toward a "new world order." This will consist of a one-world political system, a one-world economy, and a one-world religion.

THE STARTING LINEUP

Revelation 12–13 are perhaps the most significant and detailed chapters in the New Testament in regard to understanding end-time prophecies. In these chapters the major players in the events at the end of the world are identified.

1. *Israel*

> A great and wondrous sign appeared in heaven: a woman clothed with the sun, with the moon under her feet and a crown of twelve stars on her head.   *Revelation 12:1*

One scholar states that the identity of this woman is "the most critical issue in properly interpreting the Apocalypse."[2] The key to understanding her identity lies in the fact that she gives birth to a son, "who will rule all the nations with an iron scepter" (v. 5). This is a clear reference to Jesus Christ and his future kingdom. Who is this woman? Either she is the Virgin Mary, or this is a symbolic reference to the nation of Israel—through whom Messiah came. Further study indicates that the woman represents Israel. She is driven into the wilderness for three and a half years and suffers great tribulation. She is given wings like an eagle to fly away to a serene place. Some scholars see in the eagle a reference to a special airlift. Others see a reference to the United States, whose national symbol is an eagle and who has been a political protector of Israel since 1948. The point is that, in either case, God protects Israel.

2. *Satan*

> Then another sign appeared in heaven: an enormous red dragon with seven heads and ten horns and seven crowns on his heads.   *Revelation 12:3*

The dragon represents Satan. He is "that ancient serpent called the devil or Satan, who leads the whole world astray" (v. 9). Near the end of the world, Satan is refused access to heaven and goes down to the earth "filled with fury, because he knows that his time is short" (v. 12). He makes war against the woman and her offspring (v. 17). During this time there will be a dramatic upsurge in satanic activity (v. 9). This will include demon worship and increased murders, drug addiction, sexual immorality, and theft (Revelation 9:20–21).

3. *Jesus Christ*

She gave birth to a son, a male child, who will rule all the
nations with an iron scepter. And her child was snatched up
to God and to his throne.   *Revelation 12:5*

Note that during the events predicted in these chapters, the
male child—Jesus Christ—is not present on the earth. Rather, he
is in the presence of God and his throne, having been "taken up"
in his ascension (Acts 1:9) and exaltation (Philippians 2:9–11).
However, this does not mean that Christ is unconcerned with and
detached from the events on planet Earth. On the contrary, he is
very much involved. He was the only one found worthy to open
the seven-sealed scroll and initiate the terrible events of the tribulation period. He is the one who will return to earth, defeat Satan
and his armies, and establish his kingdom of peace (Revelation
19:11–16).

4. *Michael and his angels*

And there was war in heaven. Michael and his angels
fought against the dragon, and the dragon and his angels
fought back.   *Revelation 12:7*

Along with the terrible events and conflicts on the earth during the tribulation period, there will also be cosmic conflict in
heaven. Michael and his angels will do battle with Satan and his
angels. Satan will be thrown out of heaven. We know from Scripture that Satan has already fallen and was ejected from heaven, but
he still has access to God's presence when he accuses the community of faith (v. 10). As we approach the end of the world, Satan
will be permanently disbarred from heaven and will, in turn, focus
all his anger and power against Israel. The Tribulation is a specific
time when all the powers of Satan and his demons are loosed on
the earth.

5. *The believers*

Then the dragon was enraged at the woman and went off
to make war against the rest of her offspring—those who

obey God's commandments and hold to the testimony of
Jesus.   *Revelation 12:17*

This verse refers to Jewish believers during the tribulation
period. Even though they are oppressed and harassed by Satan,
they remain true to God's commandments and Jesus Christ. During this time God sends out 144,000 "servants" who are apparently
preachers of the gospel (Revelation 7:3–4). As a result of their
ministry, a large number of people become believers. "These are
they who have come out of the great tribulation; they have washed
their robes and made them white in the blood of the Lamb" (Revelation 7:14).

6. *The Antichrist*

And the dragon stood on the shore of the sea. And I saw
a beast coming out of the sea. He had ten horns and seven
heads, with ten crowns on his horns, and on each head a blasphemous name.   *Revelation 13:1*

The description of this beast is similar to Daniel's description of the Roman Empire and the coming Antichrist. He is like a
leopard, bear, and lion (Daniel 7). He has seven heads and ten
horns. This is what we read about him:

a. He is empowered by Satan (Revelation 13:2)
b. He is healed of a fatal wound (v. 3)
c. The whole world sees this miracle (v. 3)
d. People worship Antichrist (v. 4)
e. No one can oppose his military power (v. 4)
f. He will experience authority for three and a half years
   (v. 5)
g. He will blaspheme God (v. 6)
h. He will go to war against the saints (v. 7)

7. *The False Prophet*

Then I saw another beast, coming out of the earth. He had
two horns like a lamb, but he spoke like a dragon. He exercised all the authority of the first beast on his behalf, and

made the earth and its inhabitants worship the first beast, whose fatal wound had been healed. *Revelation 13:11–12*

I believe that the second beast is the false prophet who is judged along with the Antichrist (the first beast) and Satan (Revelation 20:7–10). The second beast is different from the first in that it comes from the earth instead of the sea, but the two work in intimate cooperation, as in international affairs. The second beast will do the following:

a. Cause the earth to worship Antichrist (Revelation 13:12)
b. Perform miraculous deeds "in full view of men" (v. 13)
c. Set up an image of the Antichrist and then bring the image to life (vv. 14–15)
d. Establish a world economy requiring everyone to bear the "mark," or "number," of the beast (666) in order to survive (vv. 16–18)

THE UNHOLY TRINITY

During the tribulation period an unholy trinity will dominate the world—Satan, the Antichrist, and the False Prophet. The Antichrist and the False Prophet will be the visible players, while Satan will be orchestrating world events behind the scenes. The Bible predicts that the activities and power of Satan will increase greatly at this time.

First, the restraining influence of the church and the Holy Spirit will be gone because of the rapture of the church. Today the church and individual believers have a positive influence on culture. We act as salt and light. We oppose the influence of Satan and restrain the advance of evil. But when we are removed from the scene, Satan will be free of the restraints and evil will advance for the most part unopposed (2 Thessalonians 2:6).

Second, the Bible predicts that during the Tribulation, hoards of demons who are now imprisoned in the Abyss will be released to wreak havoc on the earth. Many people will actually worship these demons (Revelation 9:1–6; 20–21).

The unholy trinity of Satan, the Antichrist, and the False Prophet will together reshape the world as we know it. They will establish a one-world government, a one-world economy, and a one-world religion. They will be the undisputed leaders of a true global village.

A ONE-WORLD GOVERNMENT

Even a casual observer of geopolitical trends can see that we are already moving toward international cooperation and interdependence. The idea of a world-governing body to which individual nations belong is no longer an exotic idea, but has increasing acceptance among the nations of the world. There are at least two compelling reasons for this trend.

First, the increasing complexities of our world serve as a catalyst to enhance our desire for international cooperation and understanding. No individual nation or superpower can any longer mediate the conflicts or resolve the problems among us. It will demand a transcendent power to which all nations will submit. In his book *The Omega Generation*, Nate Krupp identifies five major global problems that can be solved only with the help of a one-world government.

1. How to prevent wars from occurring
2. How to have enough food to feed all the people of the world
3. How to stop, or a least control, the arms race, particularly nuclear weapons
4. How to provide adequate fuel, especially oil, for the needs of the world
5. How to redistribute the world's wealth of money and material so that all will have ample supply[3]

These issues will continue to plague the human community. Resolving them will demand worldwide cooperation and a willingness to forfeit national interests for the sake of global interests. A one-world government would be the most viable institution through which to resolve these compelling problems.

Second, the United Nations already serves as an institutional micro-model of what could potentially occur on a wider scale. The United Nations was formed to deal precisely with the kinds of problems Krupp identifies. The Charter of the United Nations was signed at the San Francisco Conference on June 26, 1945. It states:

WE THE PEOPLE OF THE UNITED NATIONS
DETERMINED

to save succeeding generations from the scourge of war, which twice in our lifetime has brought untold sorrow to mankind, and

to reaffirm faith in fundamental human rights, in the dignity and worth of the human person, in the equal rights of men and women and of nations large and small, and

to establish conditions under which justice and respect for the obligations arising from treaties and other sources of international law can be maintained, and

to promote social progress and better standards of life in larger freedom.

AND FOR THESE ENDS

to practice tolerance and live together in peace with one another as good neighbors, and

to unite our strength to maintain international peace and security and

to ensure, by the acceptance of principles and the institution of methods, that armed force shall not be used, save in the common interest, and

to employ international machinery for the promotion of the economic and social advancement of all peoples.

HAVE RESOLVED TO COMBINE OUR EFFORTS
TO ACCOMPLISH THESE AIMS.

Accordingly, our respective Governments, through representatives assembled in the city of San Francisco, who have exhibited their full powers found to be in good and due form, have agreed to the present Charter of the United Nations and do hereby establish an international organization to be known as the United Nations.[4]

Article 1 of the Purposes and Principles of the Charter clearly identifies the specific goals of the ongoing action.

The Purposes of the United Nations are:

1. To maintain international peace and security, and to that end: to take effective collective measures for the prevention and removal of threats to the peace, and for the suppression of acts of aggression or other breaches of the peace, and to bring about by peaceful means, and in conformity with the principles of justice and international law adjustment or settlement of international disputes or situations which might lead to a breach of the peace;

2. To develop friendly relations among nations based on respect for the principle of equal rights and self-determination of peoples, and to take other appropriate measures to strengthen universal peace;

3. To achieve international cooperation in solving international problems of an economic, social, cultural, or humanitarian character, and in promoting and encouraging respect for human rights and for fundamental freedoms for all without distinction as to race, sex, language, or religion; and

4. To be a center for harmonizing the actions of nations in the attainment of these common ends.[5]

After the formation of the United Nations, many Christians wrote, spoke, and taught against it. Some Christians felt it was the beginning step toward a one-world government headed by the Antichrist. Therefore it was aligned with Satan and should be opposed. Others felt it was another human attempt to build the tower of Babel and, as a result, was doomed to failure. A popular painting in a number of Christian homes showed the United Nations Building in New York City with a giant Jesus knocking at the door; it symbolized the exclusion of Christ and God from the world body.

But the United Nations has survived those attacks and is stronger today than ever before. Is it of Satan? Is it another tower of Babel? Very unlikely. It is a sincere attempt to promote peace and security in an increasingly troubled world. Is it the embryonic organization that will lead to a one-world government? Possibly— but that does not make it morally evil. The Antichrist and Satan will use already established political systems to advance their cause. That does not mean that these systems, if they already exist, should be opposed by Christians. We ought to be promoters of peace (Matthew 5:9). The coming one-world government is presumably either an extension of the United Nations or modeled after the pattern and purpose of the United Nations. In either case, we are already operating with transnational interests in mind. The stage is already set for the future one-world government.

A ONE-WORLD ECONOMY

He also forced everyone, small and great, rich and poor, free and slave, to receive a mark on his right hand or on his forehead, so that no one could buy or sell unless he had the mark, which is the name of the beast or the number of his name.

This calls for wisdom. If anyone has insight, let him calculate the number of the beast, for it is man's number. His number is 666.   *Revelation 13:16–18*

The Antichrist and the False Prophet will establish not only a one-world government, but also a one-world economy. Along with the current trend toward political fusion there is also an economic one. The Bible predicts such a global economy—one so tightly controlled that no one will be able to buy or sell without the mark 666.

The significance of 666. There has been much speculation over the years about the significance of this number, and many have attempted to identify it with a specific person or thing. Most of this speculation involves assigning numerical value to letters and adding those values together. Take, for example, the name of a former president, Ronald Wilson Reagan. Each of the names has six letters; align them, and we have 666. Of course, the same could be done with my own name: Edward (6 letters) George (6 letters) Dobson (6 letters).

Others have developed more sophisticated methods of identifying the Antichrist and his mark. For example, we could establish an alphabet using multiples of 6.

A=6   F=36   K=66   P=96   U=126   Z=156
B=12   G=42   L=72   Q=102   V=132
C=18   H=48   M=78   R=108   W=138
D=24   I=54   N=84   S=114   X=144
E=30   J=60   O=90   T=120   Y=150

Take the word C O M P U T E R:

C = 18
O = 90
M = 78
P = 96
U = 126
T = 120
E = 30
R = 108

COMPUTER = 666[6]

The truth is that no one knows for sure the full significance or application of this sign. At best, it appears to be associated with human wisdom and ability in contrast to dependence on God. It entails a system that ignores God.

The controlling power of the mark of the beast. Placing the mark of the beast on either the right hand or the forehead is the means by which the government—that is, the Antichrist and the False Prophet—will control commerce around the world. Several conditions will emerge when these events occur.

- There will be a loss of personal freedom and the invasion of privacy.
- The government will control people's lives, including the basic issues of buying food and nourishment.

- There will be worldwide registration so that every person can be monitored and tracked.
- Radicals who refuse registration with the government will be eliminated.

At one time this kind of talk seemed futurist and foolish—but no longer. In the *New York Times Magazine*, Robert Ellis Smith expresses alarm at the growing interest in issuing a national ID card to everyone living in the United States. The climate of the culture and society is precipitating this interest. Smith writes, "Faced with rising crime, illegal immigration, welfare fraud and absentee parents, many bureaucrats and members of Congress insist that the nation would run more smoothly if we all had counterfeit-proof plastic identity cards."[7] What would this card do? "It would make it easy to track illicit cash transactions, to discover after the fact all persons at the scene of a crime, to know immediately whether an adult accompanying a child is a parent or legal guardian, to keep a list of suspicious persons in a neighborhood each night, to know who purchased a gun or knife or fertilizer or Satanic books, or to know who carries the H.I.V. virus."[8]

One can immediately see positive benefits from a national ID: the ability to track criminals, guarantee security, and eliminate violence.

In addition to a national ID, many are advocating a cashless society. Think of what this would do to the drug trade—without cash you could not buy or sell drugs. For ordinary commerce, think of the convenience of making all your transactions with a card. It is entirely possible that the national ID and a credit card would be the same. Furthermore, the technology is already available to use computer-readable implants that would replace plastic cards and IDs. Lawrence N. Gold has written about "devices that can be carried, worn—or even implanted under the skin. These sensors will store and transmit data . . . identifying not only who is in the room, but also his or her physiological state in response to both TV programs and advertising messages."[9]

The technology is already available to place a mark on the hand or forehead, as the Bible indicates. Smith's article has a photograph showing a man from the neck up, with his back to the camera. On the back of his neck is a bar code such as we see on products in the store—and beneath it on his neck is the number 78236D1230. Again, a cashless society is not morally evil, nor is talk about a national ID card. Many uses of that technology could be beneficial. However, the net result would be the loss of privacy and the potential dehumanizing of people. Moreover, the system could ultimately be exploited by the Antichrist to control the world's population.

A ONE-WORLD RELIGION

Religion has always played a major role in world affairs. During the tribulation period, religion will play a part in the Antichrist's program and the new world order. Out of the diverse and hostile history of religion will come the hope and desire for the reality of a one-world faith. Christians have long speculated about this religion. A popular view among some Protestants is that the one-world church is the Roman Catholic Church and the pope is either the Antichrist or the False Prophet. This view was popularized by the early Reformers who were reacting to the teaching and practices of the Roman church. John Wycliffe (1329–1384) declared that the Antichrist is the pope. Martin Luther (1483–1546) thought so, too.[10]

This view was the predominant opinion that I heard growing up in Belfast, Northern Ireland. Of course, this view reflected the enduring conflict between Protestants and Catholics in that country. However, it does not hold up under the scrutiny of Scripture. The Catholic Church could not be the one-world church, nor could the pope be the Antichrist—because of what they believe. The "spirit" of Antichrist that will prevail at the end of the world is one that denies the deity of Jesus Christ (1 John 4:1–3). Whatever you may think of the Roman Catholic Church, one thing is certain: It does *not* deny the deity of Jesus Christ. Therefore it could never be associated with the Antichrist. It fails the test of denying Jesus.

Students of biblical prophecy have variously speculated that the one-world religion is everything from Islam to the World Council of Churches to Eastern religions and New Age thinking. However, the pragmatic reality is that it is highly unlikely that any current major world religion would give up its distinctives and embrace some kind of synthetic religion. Is it reasonable to believe that Islam would find common ground with Hinduism and that both would be submerged voluntarily into a common belief system? Given the rising tide of religious zealotry in the world, this appears impossible.

Then what does the Bible mean when it predicts a one-world religion? In my opinion, it may be similar to the one-world government. The one-world government will recognize individual nations, but these nations will cooperate voluntarily for the greater good of the human race. A similar structure could emerge that will permit each religion to exist as a specific identity and at the same time participate in an "assembly" of world religions in which the common good of the human race has the highest priority. According to the report called *Global 2000 Revisited,* this is precisely what is needed to deal with the complex geopolitical situations facing the world in the twenty-first century. This report argues that we must create a more healthy and balanced world by working together with these objectives:

a. create the religious, social, and economic conditions necessary to stop the growth of human population;

b. reduce the use of resources (sources) and disposal capacity (sinks) by the wealthiest;

c. ensure civil order, education, and health services for people everywhere;

d. preserve soils and species everywhere;

e. double agricultural yields while reducing both agricultural dependence on energy and agricultural damage to the environment;

   f. convert from carbon dioxide-emitting energy sources to renewable, non-polluting energy sources that are affordable even to the poor;

   g. cut sharply the emissions of other greenhouse gases;

   h. stop immediately the emissions of the chemicals destroying the ozone layer; and

   i. bring equity between nations and peoples of the North and South.[11]

This report asserts that the task of dealing with these issues is "fundamentally spiritual in nature." In other words, religion must lead the way, and in order to lead the way there must be cooperation among the world religions. The report suggests a number of religious questions that need to be addressed.

What are the traditional teachings—and the range of other opinions—within your faith on the meaning of "progress" and how it is to be achieved?

What does your faith tradition teach about the human destiny? Is the human destiny separable from that of Earth?

What is your destiny, the destiny of the followers of your faith tradition? What does your tradition teach concerning the destiny of followers of other traditions?

How are we to measure "progress"? Can there be progress for the human community without progress for the whole community of life?

How is personal "success" related to "progress" for the whole?

What are the traditional teachings—and the range of other opinions—within your faith tradition concerning a proper relationship with those who differ in race or gender (conditions one cannot change), or culture, politics, or faith?

Much hatred and violence is carried out in the name of religion. What teachings of your faith tradition have been used—correctly or not—in an attempt to justify such practices?

Discrimination and even violence by men toward women is often justified in the name of religion. Which, if any, of the teachings of your faith have been used—correctly or incorrectly—in this way?

How does your faith tradition characterize the teachings and followers of other faiths? Do some adherents of your tradition hold that the teachings and followers of other faiths are evil, dangerous, misguided? Is there any possibility that your faith tradition can derive wisdom, truth, or insight from the teaching of another faith?

What are the traditional teachings—and the range of other opinions—within your faith on the possibility of criticism, correction, reinterpretation, and even rejection of ancient traditional assumptions and "truth" in light of new understandings or revelations?

Does your faith tradition envision new revelation, new understanding, new interpretation, new wisdom, and new truth concerning human activity affecting the future of Earth?[12]

It is conceivable that the complex problems that threaten the survival of the human race will force religions to work together toward solutions. Like the United Nations, there could also be a United Religious Assembly. Working together for political and spiritual goals under the gifted leadership of Antichrist, the world would enter a new phase of cooperation and progress.

THE NEW WORLD ORDER

The Bible clearly predicts a shift toward one-world government, economy, and religion. This globalism will be used by the Antichrist to control the world. These trends are already under way. More and more as we approach the end of the world, these same three trends will be accelerated.

Chapter 6

THE RISE AND FALL OF THE ANTICHRIST

When I was born on December 30, 1949, in a thatched cottage outside Magherafelt, Northern Ireland, my parents named me Edward George. Both names have significance. They were the first names of my grandfathers, who in turn were named for the British king who was on the throne when they were born. In the Bible, nearly all names and titles have immense significance. One name important to our understanding of the future is "the Antichrist."

The Bible predicts that as we approach the end of the world, chaos, instability, and disorder will increase. Jesus foretold that there would be "wars and rumors of wars. . . . Nation will rise against nation, and kingdom against kingdom. There will be famines and earthquakes in various places" (Matthew 24:6–7). The Bible also predicts that this chaos will give rise to a geopolitical climate that will pave the way for the rise of a new world leader who will be able to negotiate world peace and deliver on the promise of security and harmony. This world leader is a person whom most Bible students call the Antichrist.

IT'S ALL IN THE NAME

Even though that person is called the Antichrist in only one passage in the Bible (1 John 2:18–22), the name is most appropriate because it describes his essential character. He is, indeed, anti Christ. Whatever Christ is for, the Antichrist is against. Christ is light, life, and love; the Antichrist is darkness, death, and hatred. The Antichrist embodies all that is evil and opposed to God. His mission on planet Earth is to destroy.

Even though the name appears only once, references to the Antichrist appear throughout the Bible under various titles and descriptions of his character. These names and titles include the following:[1]

1. The Little Horn

"While I was thinking about the horns, there before me was another horn, a little one, which came up among them; and three of the first horns were uprooted before it. This horn had eyes like the eyes of a man and a mouth that spoke boastfully."   *Daniel 7:8*

2. The Insolent King

"In the latter part of their reign, when rebels have become completely wicked, a stern-faced king, a master of intrigue, will arise."   *Daniel 8:23*

3. The Prince Who Is to Come

"After the sixty-two 'sevens,' the Anointed One will be cut off and will have nothing. The people of the ruler who will come will destroy the city and the sanctuary."

Daniel 9:26

4. The One Who Makes Desolate

"So when you see standing in the holy place 'the abomination that causes desolation,' spoken of through the prophet Daniel—let the reader understand."   *Matthew 24:15*

5. The Man of Lawlessness

Don't let anyone deceive you in any way, for that day will
not come until the rebellion occurs and the man of lawlessness is revealed, the man doomed to destruction.

2 Thessalonians 2:3

6. The Man of Destruction

Don't let anyone deceive you in any way, for that day will
not come until the rebellion occurs and the man of lawlessness is revealed, the man doomed to destruction.

2 Thessalonians 2:3

7. The Lawless One

And then the lawless one will be revealed, whom the Lord
Jesus will overthrow with the breath of his mouth and destroy
by the splendor of his coming.   *2 Thessalonians 2:8*

8. The Beast

And I saw a beast coming out of the sea. He had ten horns
and seven heads, with ten crowns on his horns, and on each
head a blasphemous name.   *Revelation 13:1*

9. The Despicable Person

"He will be succeeded by a contemptible person who has
not been given the honor of royalty. He will invade the kingdom when its people feel secure, and he will seize it through
intrigue."   *Daniel 11:21*

10. The Strong-willed King

"The king will do as he pleases. He will exalt and mag-
nify himself above every god and will say unheard-of things
against the God of gods. He will be successful until the time
of wrath is completed, for what has been determined must
take place."   *Daniel 11:36*

11. The Worthless Shepherd

"For I am going to raise up a shepherd over the land who
will not care for the lost, or seek the young, or heal the

injured, or feed the healthy, but will eat the meat of the choice sheep, tearing off their hoofs.

"Woe to the worthless shepherd, who deserts the flock! May the sword strike his arm and his right eye! May his arm be completely withered, his right eye totally blinded!"

Zechariah 11:16–17

HIS RISE TO POWER

We saw in chapter 4 that Daniel had a dream that centered around four beasts—a lion, a bear, a leopard, and an unnamed beast (Daniel 7:1–28). These four beasts represent four major world empires, parallel with the kingdoms described in Nebuchadnezzar's dream recorded in Daniel 3. In both cases, the greatest attention is given to the fourth one—the Roman Empire—which is predicted to exist in several phases.

Phase 1: After the collapse of the Greek Empire, the Roman Empire will emerge and rule the world (see Daniel 7:23).

Phase 2: The second phase will take the form of a political coalition among the different nations and kings—nations that lie within the original boundaries of the Roman Empire (v. 24).

Phase 3: The third phase will be marked by the rise of "another king," who will form a coalition with three of the ten kings. Because of the way he is described, most scholars believe that this is a reference to the rise of the Antichrist. He will oppose God, persecute believers, change the laws, and persecute the saints for three and one-half years (vv. 24–25). The Antichrist will eventually take leadership of the entire ten-king coalition and from this power base gain worldwide authority.

THE ANTICHRIST: GENTILE OR JEW?

Because the Antichrist comes to power through a revived European community, it is most likely that he will be of European origin. Students of biblical prophecy have long debated whether he will have Jewish roots. The Antichrist will forge a peace treaty that helps to resolve the Jewish-Arab conflict. The Jewish nation will agree to this treaty, or covenant, and some argue that it would be more likely for the Jews to trust another Jew rather than a Gentile with their security and future. However, there is no clear biblical support for the idea that the Antichrist has Jewish roots.

Thus, I find it more probable that the Antichrist will be a Gentile. First, the Syrian king Antiochus Epiphanes (Daniel 11) is the clear prototype of the Antichrist, and he was a Gentile. Second, the time period leading up to the Tribulation and the end of the world is called "the times of the Gentiles" (Luke 21:24), and the Antichrist will be the undisputed ruler of the gentile world.

HIS RESUME

The book of Daniel and the book of Revelation give us the most insight into the Antichrist. A careful study of these books along with several other passages reveals some of his distinctive characteristics.

1. *He will be opposed to God*. This is the predominant characteristic of the Antichrist. This opposition is not only implied in his name, but also identified as his major mission. "He will speak against the Most High" (Daniel 7:25)—that is, he will be opposed to God and also seek to become God. "He will oppose and will exalt himself over everything that is called God or is worshiped, so that he sets himself up in God's temple, proclaiming himself to be God" (2 Thessalonians 2:4).

2. *He will try to change natural law and moral law*. The Antichrist will "try to change the set times and laws" (Daniel 7:25). The old paradigms centered on the old laws will become invalid. New paradigms based on new laws will emerge. From a biblical perspective, these new paradigms and new laws will be anti-God and anti-biblical. The net effect of these new laws will be lawlessness (2 Thessalonians 2:3).

3. *He will emerge on the scene as a man of peace*. Revelation 6:2 introduces the Antichrist as one riding on a white horse. He will initially bring peace to the world by forging a treaty in the Middle East. But the peace will not be permanent, and eventually

the Antichrist will marshal the forces of evil for the final battle against Israel, called the Battle of Armageddon.

4. *He will be nonreligious.* The Antichrist will be the ultimate humanist and secularist. "He will show no regard for the gods of his fathers, . . . nor will he regard any god" (Daniel 11:37). He will break from the traditions of the past and show no preference for religion of any kind. This could be the very reason he will be embraced and trusted by the religions of the world. But soon his religious agenda will emerge, and he will persecute and harass the saints.

5. *He will possess overwhelming military power.* The god that matters to the Antichrist is not religious in nature, but military. That is, he will worship the god of military strength and power. "He will honor a god of fortresses" (Daniel 11:38)—a reference to a place of military power. The Antichrist will spend immense amounts of money to acquire this power (v. 38) and then use it to defeat other national military powers (v. 39). He will form coalitions to advance his objective of world leadership (v. 39). His military might will be undisputed. "Who is like the beast? Who can make war against him?" (Revelation 13:4).

6. *He will realign national boundaries and material resources.* Those who align themselves with the Antichrist will be rewarded. They will be given political power (Daniel 11:39) but also land, which seems to imply a reordering of national boundaries and a restructuring of national wealth. It appears that the whole world will be turned upside down under the Antichrist.

7. *He will proclaim himself as God.* The Antichrist will proclaim himself as God (2 Thessalonians 2:4). This idea may seem far-fetched in the sophisticated world in which we live, but actually it is not. There is widespread intellectual acceptance of the concept of humans being god. Philosophical humanism as a system essentially deifies human beings. It was developed by the pre-Socratic philosopher Protagoras, who coined the phrase "man is the measure of all things." Mankind is the center of the universe, not God. Mankind establishes morals and values. The logical conclusion is that God is unnecessary, if he exists at all.

Humanism is the underlying intellectual foundation of what we call "modern thinking"—the scientific age, the age of empiricism, the age of rationalism, the Enlightenment. Humanism is a philosophy or attitude that addresses itself exclusively to the human as opposed to the divine or the supernatural; it is often accompanied by a belief that we are capable of reaching self-fulfillment without divine aid. That may be an oversimplification of humanist philosophy, but the bottom line is that we really don't need God. It is up to us to improve society. We must educate people. And all we need is ourselves, science, and our own ability and creativity.

Could it be that the Antichrist is the ultimate expression and the highest ideal of humanistic philosophy? He will be a person possessed of incredible intellectual ability who appears to be the ultimate expression of everything that is good about humanity—and offers the world peace without God. In the words of John Lennon's song, "A world with no religion too." We don't need God. We don't need religion. All we need is ourselves.

New Age religion, which is spreading through the Western world, also raises the prospect of worshiping the Antichrist as a god. It has its roots in Eastern religion and pantheism, the teaching that "all is God, God is all." We are all gods. God is the tree and the bird. New Age religion is the journey to discover the god who is within us. Will the Antichrist be the guru of New Age thinking, the ultimate expression of God?

Given these philosophical currents in Western society, it is not hard to imagine a time when someone comes onto the stage of history possessing brilliant diplomatic skills and impressive credentials and declaring, "The problem with the world is religion. It is Jew and Arab. It is Muslim and Christian. It is Catholic and Protestant. The problem of the world is God. We don't need God. We only need our own capability. After all, we are god. We are the measure of all things. We're the ones who determine our fate and our future." And the world turns to this imposing individual and says, "You know, you're right. We are somebody. We possess the ability to alter society forever. We can bring peace into the world."

Turning from organized religion, the world proclaims this individual as the ultimate savior of humanity—a god.

THE ANTICHRIST AND ISRAEL

A prominent prediction concerning the Antichrist is that he will make a "covenant," or treaty, with the State of Israel for seven years (Daniel 9:27).

Several related historical events surround this prediction by Daniel.

- Israel will exist as a nation in the land.
- There will be a compelling need for peace in the Middle East and therefore the need for a treaty.
- The temple in Jerusalem will be partially or completely rebuilt.
- The Levitical system of sacrifices and offerings will be reestablished.

Halfway through this period, he will break the treaty and abolish the offerings and sacrifices at the temple in Jerusalem. He will also desecrate the temple and begin persecuting the Jews.

THE PROTOTYPE OF THE ANTICHRIST

> Out of one of them came another horn.   *Daniel 8:9*

Many Bible scholars agree that the "horn" mentioned in this verse is Antiochus Epiphanes. Antiochus's brother, Seleucus IV Philopater, was the king of Syria but was murdered in 175 B.C. Seleucus's son, Demetrius, was the rightful heir to the throne, but he was being held hostage in Rome. Amid this political turmoil and intrigue, Antiochus seized the throne. He added the word "Epiphanes" to his title, which means "the illustrious one." Antiochus not only holds a prominent place in Mideastern history, but is also a prototype of the future Antichrist.

1. *His rise to power*

> Out of one of them came another horn, which started small but grew in power to the south and to the east and toward the Beautiful Land.   *V. 9*

This verse tells us that Antiochus conquered land to the south (Egypt), to the east (Armenia), and the "Beautiful Land" (Palestine). The ancient historical records of Antiochus Epiphanes describe battles in all these regions.

2. *His oppression*

> It grew until it reached the host of the heavens, and it threw some of the starry host down to the earth and trampled on them.
>   *V. 10*

What does it mean that after conquering all those territories, Antiochus Epiphanes reached the "host of the heavens" and threw down some of the stars and trampled them? I believe this is a metaphorical way of saying that he oppressed the Jewish people. The stars of heaven represent the Jews.

> Then the word of the LORD came to him: "This man will not be your heir, but a son coming from your own body will be your heir." He took him outside and said, "Look up at the heavens and count the stars—if indeed you can count them." Then he said to him, "So shall your offspring be."
>   *Genesis 15:4–5*

Antiochus opposed the Jews and began to harass and persecute them. The terror of these days is recorded in the book of the Maccabees.

> There were also seven brothers who were arrested with their mother. The king tried to force them to taste pig's flesh, which the Law forbids, by torturing them with whips and scourges. One of them, acting as spokesman for the others, said, "What are you trying to find out from us? We are prepared to die rather than break the laws of our ancestors." The king, in a fury, ordered pans and cauldrons to be heated over a fire. As soon as they were red-hot he commanded that this spokesman of theirs should have his tongue cut out, his head scalped and his extremities cut off, while the other brothers and his mother looked on. When he had been rendered completely helpless, the king gave orders for him to be brought, still breathing, to the fire and fried alive in a pan. As the smoke

from the pan drifted about, his mother and the rest encouraged one another to die nobly, with such words as these, "The Lord God is watching, and surely he takes pity on us, as in the song in which Moses bore witness against the people to their face, proclaiming that 'he will certainly take pity on his servants.'"   *2 Maccabees 7:1–6 JB*

3. *His desolation*

It set itself up to be as great as the Prince of the host; it took away the daily sacrifice from him, and the place of his sanctuary was brought low. Because of rebellion, the host of the saints and the daily sacrifice were given over to it. It prospered in everything it did, and truth was thrown to the ground.
                                                    Daniel 8:11–12

Antiochus elevated himself to the stature of a god. He had coins minted that bore the inscription *Theos Antiochus, Theos Epiphanes,* which means "God Antiochus—God manifest." He banned sacrifices at the temple and desecrated the altar instead by offering pigs for sacrifices. The book of the Maccabees describes these dark days.

Then the king issued a proclamation to his whole kingdom that all were to become a single people, each renouncing his particular customs. All the pagans conformed to the king's decree, and many Israelites chose to accept his religion, sacrificing to idols and profaning the sabbath. The king also sent instructions by messenger to Jerusalem and the towns of Judah directing them to adopt customs foreign to the country, banning holocausts, sacrifices and libations from the sanctuary, profaning sabbaths and feasts, defiling the sanctuary and the sacred ministers, building altars, precincts and shrines for idols, sacrificing pigs and unclean beasts, leaving their sons uncircumcised, and prostituting themselves to all kinds of impurity and abomination, so that they should forget the Law and revoke all observance of it. Anyone not obeying the king's command was to be put to death. Writing in such terms to every part of his kingdom, the king appointed inspectors for the whole people, and directed all the towns of Judah to offer sacrifice one after another.   *1 Maccabees 1:41–54 JB*

4. *His defeat*

Then I heard a holy one speaking, and another holy one said to him, "How long will it take for the vision to be fulfilled—the vision concerning the daily sacrifice, the rebellion that causes desolation, and the surrender of the sanctuary and of the host that will be trampled underfoot?"

He said to me, "It will take 2,300 evenings and mornings; then the sanctuary will be reconsecrated." *Daniel 8:13–14*

"The rebellion that causes desolation" involves the desecration of the altar in the temple at Jerusalem. Antiochus created an altar to Zeus over the Jewish altar and offered unclean animals—pigs—as sacrifices. The text predicts that this desolation would last 2,300 days—approximately six years. Antiochus began his desecration in 171 B.C.

Antiochus's brazen defiance of God and the Jewish religion stirred a rebellion that finally brought about his downfall, rebellion known as the Maccabean revolt.

In those days Mattathias son of John, son of Simeon, a priest of the line of Joarib, left Jerusalem and settled in Modein. He had five sons, John known as Gaddi, Simon called Thassi, Judas called Maccabaeus, Eleazar, called Avaran, and Jonathan called Apphus. When he saw the blasphemies being committed in Judah and Jerusalem, he said, "Alas that I should have been born to witness the overthrow of my people, and the overthrow of the Holy City, and to sit by while she is delivered over to her enemies, and the sanctuary into the hand of foreigners.

"Her Temple has become like a man of no repute, the vessels that were her glory have been carried off as booty, her babies have been slaughtered in her streets, her young men by the enemy's sword. Is there a nation that has not claimed a share of her royal prerogatives, that has not taken some of her spoils? All her ornaments have been snatched from her, her former freedom has become slavery. See how our Holy

Place, our beauty, our glory, is now laid waste, profaned by the pagans. What have we left to live for?"

Mattathias and his sons tore their garments, put on sackcloth, and observed deep mourning.

The king's commissioners who were enforcing the apostasy came to the town of Modein to make them sacrifice. Many Israelites gathered round them, but Mattathias and his sons drew apart. The king's commissioners then addressed Mattathias as follows, "You are a respected leader, a great man in this town; you have sons and brothers to support you. Be the first to step forward and conform to the king's decree, as all the nations have done, and the leaders of Judah and the survivors in Jerusalem; you and your sons shall be reckoned among the Friends of the King, you and your sons shall be honoured with gold and silver and many presents." Raising his voice, Mattathias retorted, "Even if every nation living in the king's dominions obeys him, each forsaking its ancestral religion to conform to his decrees, I, my sons and my brothers will still follow the covenant of our ancestors. Heaven preserve us from forsaking the Law and its observances. As for the king's orders, we will not follow them: we will not swerve from our own religion either to right or to left." As he finished speaking, a Jew came forward in the sight of all to offer sacrifice on the altar in Modein as the royal edict required. When Mattathias saw this, he was fired with zeal; stirred to the depth of his being, he gave vent to his legitimate anger, threw himself on the man and slaughtered him on the altar. At the same time he killed the king's commissioner who was there to enforce the sacrifice and tore down the altar. In his zeal for the Law he acted as Phinehas did against Zimri son of Salu. Then Mattathias went through the town, shouting at the top of his voice, "Let everyone who has a fervour for the Law and takes his stand on the covenant come out and follow me." Then he fled with his sons into the hills, leaving all their possessions behind in the town.   *1 Maccabees 2:1–28 JB*

Shortly after this event, Mattathias died. His son, Judas, called "the Hammer," formed a band of guerrilla fighters. His tactics led to the downfall of Antiochus. Although Antiochus had

100,000 foot soldiers, 20,000 cavalry, and 32 elephants, he was no match for Judas and his guerrillas. Antiochus was forced back to Syria. Demetrius, who was the rightful king of Syria and had by this time been released from prison in Rome, was now on the throne. He arrested Antiochus and had him beheaded.

In 165 B.C. the temple was cleansed and rededicated, and the Jewish sacrifices were restored. On December 25 of that year, an eight-day celebration began, during which a candle was lit each day. This is now called the feast of Hanukkah, or festival of lights.

HISTORY REPEATS ITSELF

The rest of Daniel 8 relates how the angel Gabriel interpreted the meaning of the vision of the "horn" to Daniel. Gabriel revealed that "the vision concerns the time of the end" (v. 17) and "the distant future" (v. 26). The explanation indicates that the historical circumstances surrounding the Maccabean revolt have a parallel in the end times.

"I am going to tell you what will happen later in the time of wrath, because the vision concerns the appointed time of the end. The two-horned ram that you saw represents the kings of Media and Persia. The shaggy goat is the king of Greece, and the large horn between his eyes is the first king. The four horns that replaced the one that was broken off represent four kingdoms that will emerge from his nation but will not have the same power.

"In the latter part of their reign, when rebels have become completely wicked, a stern-faced king, a master of intrigue, will arise. He will become very strong, but not by his own power. He will cause astounding devastation and will succeed in whatever he does. He will destroy the mighty men and the holy people. He will cause deceit to prosper, and he will consider himself superior. When they feel secure, he will destroy many and take his stand against the Prince of princes. Yet he will be destroyed, but not by human power."   *Daniel 8:19–25*

Antiochus Epiphanes is a prototype of the Antichrist. The final master of intrigue is described in some unusual terms. He will become strong, but not by his own power—probably a reference to the power of Satan. He will persecute the holy people. He will elevate himself as a god and will desecrate the temple. He will be destroyed, but not by human power—a reference to divine intervention, that is, the second coming of Christ.

THE DEFEAT OF THE ANTICHRIST

After the Antichrist forges the peace treaty with Israel, a coalition that includes Egypt and Syria threatens Israel's security (Daniel 11:40). The Antichrist defends Israel and repels these coalition forces (Ezekiel 38–39). Then another coalition forms that includes an army of two million from the east (Daniel 11:44). This army, along with help from the north, moves against Israel with the objective of annihilating the Jews. Eventually the Antichrist joins these forces, and thus the stage is set for the coming of Jesus Christ to defeat these armies in the mother of all battles: Armageddon.

> Then I saw the beast and the kings of the earth and their armies gathered together to make war against the rider on the horse and his army. But the beast was captured, and with him the false prophet who had performed the miraculous signs on his behalf. With these signs he had deluded those who had received the mark of the beast and worshiped his image. The two of them were thrown alive into the fiery lake of burning sulfur. The rest of them were killed with the sword that came out of the mouth of the rider on the horse, and all the birds gorged themselves on their flesh.   *Revelation 19:19–21*

Chapter 7

THE GREAT TRIBULATION

Independence Day is one of those movies that keeps you on the edge of your seat. From the arrival of the alien spaceships through the destruction of major cites to the final conflict, your heart pounds. As I watched the movie, I was struck by the utter chaos and breakdown of societal structure in the face of uncontrollable circumstances. Despite all its technological resources, political structures, and nuclear military power, the United States was incapable of stopping the onslaught of the alien invaders.

The film brought to mind a future time when the entire world will be incapable of dealing with a situation that goes out of control. In that day, panic, fear, and chaos will reign in people's hearts. There will be a seven-year period of "great distress, unequaled from the beginning of the world until now" (Matthew 24:21). Jesus warned that "if those days had not been cut short, no one would survive" (v. 22).

THE OLD TESTAMENT AND THE GREAT TRIBULATION

Throughout the Old Testament the prophets predicted a future time on earth when God would pour out his wrath and there would be greater distress and trouble than ever before in the history of the human race. Various phrases or titles are used to describe this event, which is most widely known as the Great Tribulation. Among these names are the following:

1. *The day of vengeance*

The LORD is angry with all nations;
   his wrath is upon all their armies.
He will totally destroy them,
   he will give them over to slaughter.
Their slain will be thrown out,
   their dead bodies will send up a stench;
the mountains will be soaked with their blood. . . .

For the LORD has a day of vengeance,
   a year of retribution, to uphold Zion's cause.

Isaiah 34:2–3, 8

2. *The time of Jacob's trouble*

" 'How awful that day will be!
   None will be like it.
It will be a time of trouble for Jacob,
   but he will be saved out of it.
" 'In that day,' declares the LORD Almighty,
   'I will break the yoke off their necks
and will tear off their bonds;
   no longer will foreigners enslave them.
Instead, they will serve the LORD their God
   and David their king,
   whom I will raise up for them.' "

Jeremiah 30:7–9

3. *A time of distress*

"At the time Michael, the great prince who protects your people, will arise. There will be a time of distress such as has not happened from the beginning of nations until then. But

at that time your people—everyone whose name is found
written in the book—will be delivered."   *Daniel 12:1*

4. *The day of the* LORD

Blow the trumpet in Zion;
  sound the alarm on my holy hill.
Let all who live in the land tremble,
  for the day of the LORD *is coming.*
It is close at hand.

                                              Joel 2:1

5. *The great day of the* LORD

"The great day of the LORD *is near—*
  near and coming quickly.
Listen! The cry on the day of the LORD *will be bitter,*
  the shouting of the warrior there.
That day will be a day of wrath,
  a day of distress and anguish,
a day of trouble and ruin,
  a day of darkness and gloom,
  a day of clouds and blackness."

                                    Zephaniah 1:14–15

JESUS AND THE GREAT TRIBULATION

One of the most detailed descriptions of the Great Tribulation is found in Matthew 24. The disciples asked Jesus, "What will
be the sign of your coming and of the end of the age?" (Matthew
24:3). Jesus responded by listing many signs—not just one major
sign. Jesus described the seven years of the Tribulation as having
two parts. The first three and a half years are described in verses
4–14; the second three and a half, in verses 15–31.

The First Half

Jesus identified two kinds of signs that will point to the end
of the world and his coming: natural signs and spiritual signs.

   a. *Natural signs*

     1. Wars and rumors of wars

     2. Famines

     3. Earthquakes

   b. *Spiritual signs*

     1. False Christs

     2. Persecution against Christians

     3. Martyrdom

     4. People will turn from the faith

     5. False prophets

     6. People's love will grow cold

     7. The gospel will be preached in the whole world

These signs will be explained in chapter 10, "Fifty Remarkable Events Pointing Toward the End."

The Second Half

Jesus predicted that the second half of the Tribulation would be worse than the first. He said, "For then there will be great distress, unequaled from the beginning of the world until now—and never to be equaled again" (Matthew 24:21). Three events are predicted for this period.

   a. *The abomination of desolation* (Matthew 24:15). We saw in the previous chapter that the Antichrist will forge a peace in the Middle East and restore temple worship in Jerusalem, then later break the treaty and desecrate the temple.

   b. *Cataclysmic events in the universe*

> "Immediately after the distress of those days
>
> " '*the sun will be darkened,*
>   *and the moon will not give its light;*
> *the stars will fall from the sky,*
>   *and the heavenly bodies will be shaken.*' "
>
>   *Matthew 24:29*

We do not know whether these celestial events will be caused by human action or divine intervention. The darkening of the sun, moon, and stars may describe the aftermath of nuclear destruction, when the air is filled with dust and particles and hides the light of the sun. Or this could be the direct action of God in shaking the foundations of the universe. In either case, the events are massive in their impact.

   c. *The coming of Jesus*

> "At that time the sign of the Son of Man will appear in the sky, and all the nations of the earth will mourn. They will see the Son of Man coming on the clouds of the sky, with power and great glory. And he will send his angels with a loud trumpet call, and they will gather his elect from the four winds, from one end of the heavens to the other."
>
> *Matthew 24:30–31*

The Great Tribulation will conclude with the coming of Jesus Christ to establish his kingdom. He will come with the armies of heaven and defeat the Antichrist and his armies at the Battle of Armageddon. Jesus will then establish a worldwide kingdom with its headquarters in Jerusalem. He will then rule in peace for a thousand years.

THE BOOK OF REVELATION

Revelation, the last book of the Bible, contains the most detailed description of all regarding the end of the world, much of it expressed in symbolic terms and images. The Greek word for revelation is *apocalypsis,* from which we derive the English word *apocalypse.* We use this word to describe the end of the world or cataclysmic events such as a nuclear war. But the original Greek meaning is different: the "unveiling or revealing" of someone or something. The theme of the book of Revelation is the revealing of Jesus Christ—that is, his appearance in the Second Coming. Although the book of Revelation deals with the whole complex of events surrounding the end of the world, its primary theme is the coming of Jesus Christ.

   The book is divided into three major sections, the last being by far the longest.

> "Write, therefore, what you have seen, what is now and
> what will take place later."   *Revelation 1:19*

The first division, described by the phrase "what you have
seen," involves the vision of the writer, the apostle John, as it is
recorded in chapter 1. The second division, "what is now," contains seven messages to seven churches in Asia Minor (chapters
2–3). The third division, "what will take place later," is a prophetic
passage that covers the remaining nineteen chapters.

> At once I was in the Spirit, and there before me was a
> throne in heaven with someone sitting on it.   *Revelation 4:2*

There is no mention of the church as existing on earth during the tribulation period. Yet in the first three chapters of the book
of Revelation, the church is the central focus. In Revelation 1,
Jesus moves among the churches. In chapters 2 and 3, seven messages are delivered to seven churches. But from chapter 4 through
the end of the book, the church is not mentioned at all in regard
to the predicted events on planet Earth. What happens to the
church? I believe that between chapter 3 (the end of the church
age) and chapter 4 (the beginning of the Great Tribulation), the
church is raptured and the saints are taken to heaven.

Revelation 4 gives us a glimpse of the worship and celebration taking place in heaven after the Rapture. Chapter 5 reveals that
there is a scroll there, at God's throne, that reveals what will happen on the earth. We read that only the Lamb of God—Jesus—is
worthy to break the seven seals of the scroll and look inside.

The Seven Seals

The Tribulation begins with the opening of the scroll, one
seal at a time (6:1).

1. *The first seal: A white horse*

> I watched as the Lamb opened the first of the seven seals.
> Then I heard one of the four living creatures say in a voice
> like thunder, "Come!" I looked, and there before me was a

white horse! Its rider held a bow, and he was given a crown, and he rode out as a conqueror bent on conquest.

Revelation 6:1–2

Many Bible scholars believe that this is a reference to the Antichrist, who will emerge on the world scene offering peace— appropriately symbolized in the white horse. The Anitchrist will forge this peace with military power (a bow) and political power (a crown).

2. *The second seal: A red horse*

When the lamb opened the second seal, I heard the second living creature say, "Come!" Then another horse came out, a fiery red one. Its rider was given power to take peace from the earth and to make men slay each other. To him was given a large sword.   *Vv. 3–4*

The initial peace offered by the Antichrist is quickly broken, and war breaks out on the earth.

3. *The third seal: A black horse*

When the Lamb opened the third seal, I heard the third living creature say, "Come!" I looked, and there before me was a black horse! Its rider was holding a pair of scales in his hand. Then I heard what sounded like a voice among the four living creatures, saying, "A quart of wheat for a day's wages, and three quarts of barley for a day's wages, and do not damage the oil and the wine!"   *Vv. 5–6*

This horse represents worldwide famine. In the face of this global predicament, a few people will only get richer—there will be no damage to "the oil and the wine."

4. *The fourth seal: A pale horse*

When the Lamb opened the fourth seal, I heard the voice of the fourth living creature say, "Come!" I looked, and there before me was a pale horse! Its rider was named Death, and Hades was following close behind him. They were given power over a fourth of the earth to kill by sword, famine and plague, and by the wild beasts of the earth.   *Vv. 7–8*

The scope and depth of global problems now intensify. War, famine, disease, and natural calamity begin to take their toll of the human race. One-fourth of the population of the earth dies.

5. *The fifth seal: The martyred*

> When he opened the fifth seal, I saw under the altar the souls of those who had been slain because of the word of God and the testimony they had maintained. They called out in a loud voice, "How long, Sovereign Lord, holy and true, until you judge the inhabitants of the earth and avenge our blood?" . . . they were told to wait a little longer, until the number of their fellow servants and brothers who were to be killed as they had been was completed.   *Vv. 9–11*

The focus of the fifth seal is on events in heaven rather than on the earth. Those who had been martyred for their faith in God ask when their deaths will be avenged. They are reminded that more will yet be martyred before God brings judgment in their behalf.

6. *The sixth seal: Natural disasters*

> I watched as he opened the sixth seal. There was a great earthquake. The sun turned black like sackcloth made of goat hair, the whole moon turned blood red, and the stars in the sky fell to earth. . . . The sky receded like a scroll, rolling up, and every mountain and island was removed from its place.   *Vv. 12–14*

These disasters exceed anything this world has experienced before. They are so intense that the political leaders of the world are rendered completely helpless.

7. *The seventh seal: The seven trumpets*

> When he opened the seventh seal, there was silence in heaven for about half an hour. And I saw the seven angels who stand before God, and to them were given seven trumpets.   *Revelation 8:1–2*

The seventh seal contains seven trumpet judgments. Before they begin, however, there is silence in heaven for thirty minutes. This is the calm before the next storm.

The Seven Trumpets

> Then the seven angels who had the seven trumpets pre-
> pared to sound them.   *V. 6*

The trumpet judgments of the seventh seal are more intense than the preceding six seals.

1. *The first trumpet: The earth*

> The first angel sounded his trumpet, and there came hail and
> fire mixed with blood, and it was hurled down upon the earth.
> A third of the earth was burned up, a third of the trees were
> burned up, and all the green grass was burned up.   *V. 7*

Whether the disasters of the first trumpet are a result of nuclear destruction or a direct act of God, their effect on planet Earth is devastating.

2. *The second trumpet: The sea*

> The second angel sounded his trumpet, and something
> like a huge mountain, all ablaze, was thrown into the sea.
> A third of the sea turned into blood, a third of the living
> creatures in the sea died, and a third of the ships were
> destroyed.   *Vv. 8–9*

Here again, the description of this event suggests that it could be some form of nuclear explosion. Can you imagine the smell when one-third of the fish of the sea die?

3. *The third trumpet: The rivers*

> The third angel sounded his trumpet, and a great star,
> blazing like a torch, fell from the sky on a third of the rivers
> and on the springs of water. . . . A third of the waters turned
> bitter, and many people died from the waters that had
> become bitter.   *Vv. 10–11*

The third judgment includes a falling star named Wormwood that will poison one-third of the fresh water on the earth. As a result, many people will die.

4. *The fourth trumpet: Sun, moon, stars*

> The fourth angel sounded his trumpet, and a third of the sun was struck, a third of the moon, and a third of the stars, so that a third of them turned dark. A third of the day was without light, and also a third of the night.   *V. 12*

The judgments of God are not limited to the earth—even the sun, moon, and stars are affected. The result is a shorter day and a longer night.

These first four trumpets spell ecological and physical disaster for the planet—vegetation burned, the oceans poisoned, and the inland waters turned bitter. Even the normal cycles of day and night are altered. But the worst is yet to come.

> As I watched, I heard an eagle that was flying in midair call out in a loud voice: "Woe! Woe! Woe to the inhabitants of the earth, because of the trumpet blasts about to be sounded by the other three angels!"   *V. 13*

5. *The fifth trumpet: Demonic activity*

> The fifth angel sounded his trumpet, and I saw a star that had fallen from the sky to the earth.... The sun and sky were darkened by the smoke from the Abyss. And out of the smoke locusts came down upon the earth and were given power like that of scorpions of the earth.... During those days men will seek death, but will not find it; they will long to die, but death will elude them.   *Revelation 9:1–3, 6*

The fifth trumpet signals the beginning of increased demonic activity on the earth. The word *Abyss* means bottomless and indicates a place where many fallen demons are imprisoned (Luke 8:31; Jude 6). During the Tribulation they will be released and will torment human beings. The leader of these demons is called Abaddon in the Hebrew language and Apollyon in the Greek language. Both words mean destruction and death and refer to Satan himself.

6. *The sixth trumpet: The angels*

> The sixth angel sounded his trumpet, and I heard a voice coming from the horns of the golden altar that is before God.... And the four angels who had been kept ready for this very hour and day and month and year were released to kill a third of mankind.... A third of mankind was killed by the three plagues of fire, smoke and sulfur.   *Vv. 13, 15, 18*

A third of the world's population is killed by fire-breathing horses commanded by an army of 200 million mounted soldiers (vv. 16–17).

7. *The seventh trumpet: The Second Coming*

The events of the seventh trumpet occur in heaven, not on the earth, and culminate in the dramatic proclamation that the eternal kingdom of Christ is about to be established at last.

> The seventh angel sounded his trumpet, and there were loud voices in heaven, which said:
>
> > *"The kingdom of the world has become the kingdom*
> > *of our Lord and of his Christ,*
> > *and he will reign for ever and ever."* ...
>
> God's temple in heaven was opened, ... And there came flashes of lightning, rumblings, peals of thunder, an earthquake and a great hailstorm.   *Revelation 11:15, 19*

Miracles in the Midst of Madness

So far, the Great Tribulation appears to be nothing but gloom and doom—as indeed the term suggests. Yet, even amid these tragic events, God has those who are faithful to the truth and live as witnesses for him. These faithful include "144,000 from all the tribes of Israel" (Revelation 7:1–8) and two special people regarded as "my two witnesses" (Revelation 11:1–13).

The story of the two witnesses begins when the apostle John is commanded to measure the temple in Jerusalem during his vision. Even though the temple has been rebuilt and worship revived, the city is still under gentile influence—specifically, the power of the Antichrist who earlier forged a peace treaty with Israel. During this time, God sends two witnesses, who are like "two olive trees and the two lampstands" (v. 4). This metaphor is a reference to the ministry of Joshua and Zerubbabel, who were the high priest and the governor respectively after the Jews returned to Palestine following the Exile (Zechariah 3–4). These two were God's messengers during difficult days, and the two witnesses of the Tribulation are his messengers during the most difficult days of all.

Some believe that these two witnesses are Elijah and Enoch—the two Old Testament figures who never died. Others believe they are Moses and Elijah (Malachi 4:4–5). In either case, these men provide powerful and miraculous witness to God (Revelation 11:5–6). Eventually they are killed by Satan (v. 7) and their bodies left lying in the streets of Jerusalem. For three and a half days the entire world watches (v. 9)—and then they are miraculously raised from the dead and taken up to heaven (vv. 11–12).

This prediction about the two witnesses requires certain conditions exist before it can come to pass.

Political reality. The Jews must be inhabiting the land and occupying Jerusalem, the capital city.

Spiritual reality. The temple must have been rebuilt and worship restored.

Technological reality. The entire world must be able to see the bodies of these witnesses lying in the streets of Jerusalem.

The Severest Judgments of All

God now pours out his final and most severe judgments upon the earth. While these judgments are similar to the plagues sent on Egypt (Exodus 7:20–12:30), their severity defies explanation or understanding.

1. *The first bowl: Painful sores*

> The first angel went and poured out his bowl on the land, and ugly and painful sores broke out on the people who had the mark of the beast and worshiped his image.
>
> *Revelation 16:2*

This is a judgment against those who are part of the one-world government and the one-world religion.

2. *The second bowl: The sea*

> The second angel poured out his bowl on the sea, and it turned into blood like that of a dead man, and every living thing in the sea died.   *V. 3*

During the second trumpet judgment, one-third of the sea creatures died. Now the rest die.

3. *The third bowl: The waters*

> The third angel poured out his bowl on the rivers and springs of water, and they became blood. Then I heard the angel in charge of the waters say:
>
> *"You are just in these judgments, . . .*
> *for they have shed the blood of your saints and prophets."*
>
> *Vv. 4–6*

It appears that now all the water of the earth becomes polluted.

4. *The fourth bowl: The sun*

> The fourth angel poured out his bowl on the sun, and the sun was given power to scorch people with fire.   *V. 8*

Whether this scorching is a result of the complete depletion of the ozone layer or a direct act of God, we cannot be sure. But the effect is the same—these people are burned by the sun.

5. *The fifth bowl: Darkness*

> The fifth angel poured out his bowl on the throne of the beast, and his kingdom was plunged into darkness.
>
> *Vv. 10–11*

During this judgment, darkness descends over the entire world.

6. *The sixth bowl: The Euphrates*

> The sixth angel poured out his bowl on the great river Euphrates, and its water was dried up to prepare the way for the kings from the East.   *V. 12*

Prior to the last confrontation, the Battle of Armageddon, the River Euphrates will dry up to enable a coalition army from the East to invade Israel. This bowl judgment marks the beginning of preparations for this final battle.

7. *The seventh bowl: The greatest earthquake of all time*

> The seventh angel poured out his bowl into the air, and out of the temple came a loud voice from the throne, saying, "It is done!" Then there came flashes of lightning, rumblings, peals of thunder and a severe earthquake. No earthquake like it has ever occurred since man has been on earth, so tremendous was the quake.   *Vv. 17–18*

The last of these judgments is a mighty earthquake that affects every island and mountain in the world (v. 20). It is accompanied by a storm with hailstones up to a hundred pounds in weight (v. 21).

It is interesting to note the response of human beings to these terminal and devastating events.

> They were seared by the intense heat and they cursed the name of God, who had control over these plagues, but they refused to repent and glorify him.   *V. 9*

> Men gnawed their tongues in agony and cursed the God of heaven because of their pains and their sores, but they refused to repent of what they had done.   *Vv. 10–11*

> And they cursed God on account of the plague of hail, because the plague was so terrible.   *V. 21*

The world responds the way the Pharaoh of Egypt did to the plagues—the people harden their hearts and continue to resist God.

The Rise and Fall of Babylon

> With a mighty voice he shouted:

> *"Fallen! Fallen is Babylon the Great!*
> *She has become a home for demons*
> *and a haunt for every evil spirit,*
> *a haunt for every unclean and detestable bird."*
>   *Revelation 18:2*

Two chapters in the book of Revelation (17–18) are devoted to the fall of Babylon. The Bible has much to say about Babylon. It is first mentioned in Genesis 10:10, and the name comes from the Hebrew word *babel,* which means "the gate of God." It is the place where human beings attempted to build a tower to heaven, and as a result, God "confused" their language (Genesis 11). Babylon is mentioned in every major prophetic book—that is, the books of Isaiah, Jeremiah, Ezekiel, and Daniel.

There is a variety of interpretations as to the meaning of the name Babylon in the book of Revelation. Some believe it refers to the ancient city that was located in a region that is now part of Iraq, and therefore in the last days the city will be rebuilt and become a world center of commerce and religion. Speculation about this was fueled by Iraqi President Saddam Hussein's attempts to rebuild Babylon. Others give Babylon a symbolic interpretation. It could represent the world system that has coalesced in an economic, political, and religious partnership. It could represent the global village without God—much like the original tower of Babel (Genesis 11:1–9). For my part, I believe that the Babylon referred to in Revelation is a reference to the one-world political and religious system established by Antichrist and the false prophet. During the last days of the Tribulation, this world system will be broken.

> *"Woe! Woe, O great city,*
> *O Babylon, city of power!*
> *In one hour your doom has come!"*
> *Revelation 18:10*

The Tribulation will end with the biggest battle the earth has ever seen. The stage has been set for the Battle of Armageddon.

Chapter 8

ARMAGEDDON: THE MOTHER OF ALL BATTLES

A rmageddon. The word itself has an ominous sound to it. Webster defines the word as "the site or time of a final and conclusive battle between the forces of good and evil."[1] The word *armageddon* is a Hebrew word, the first part of which (*arm*) means "mountain" and the second part of which (*Megiddo*) refers to a specific location in northern Palestine. The literal translation of the word is "Mount Megiddo." The mountain is near the Mediterranean Sea and overlooks a valley fourteen miles wide and twenty miles long. This will be the site of the final conflict.

> Then they gathered the kings together to the place that in Hebrew is called Armageddon. *Revelation 16:16*

ARMAGEDDON AND ANTI-SEMITISM

The Battle of Armageddon will be Satan's last desperate attempt to exterminate the Jewish people and defeat the plan and purposes of God. There have been numerous attempts down through history to exterminate the Jewish people from the face of the earth. The most recent example is the Holocaust, suffered at the hands of Nazi Germany, which we described in chapter 3.

In the end times, this same kind of hatred against the Jews will lead the nations of the world to turn against Israel and make a last and final attempt to exterminate them and drive them out of the land of Palestine. That hatred festers even now and has expressed itself in two predominant ways in recent decades.

1. *The Arab-Jewish conflict.* For those who have observed the Arab-Jewish relationship over the last thirty or more years, it was an incredible moment: Yasir Arafat, the chairman of the Palestine Liberation Organization (PLO), and Yitzhak Rabin, the prime minister of Israel, shaking hands on the White House lawn on September 13, 1993. These leaders had been avowed enemies bent on each other's destruction. Now they were agreeing to recognize each other's right to exist in peace. They both looked nervous and uneasy at the ceremony, but their courageous act introduced a new phase of hope into the Arab-Jewish problem.

This was not the first time that Arab leaders and Jewish leaders had agreed to wage peace instead of war. In 1978, Anwar Sadat, the president of Egypt, and Menachem Begin, the prime minister of Israel, met with President Jimmy Carter at Camp David, Maryland. This encounter led to Sadat and Begin's signing a peace treaty later that year.

The struggle for peace in the Middle East continues. What about Jordan? What about Syria? What about the rest of the Arab nations? While the peace treaties that exist are an encouragement, they have not dramatically altered the hatred for Israel that exists in the Middle East—a hatred that has endured for more than four thousand years. We can trace it all the way back to the time of the Old Testament patriarch Abraham, who is the father of both the Arabs and the Jews. God promised to bring a great nation from Abraham and to give his family the land of Palestine (Genesis 12:1–3). But Abraham did not have a son. So rather than waiting to see how God would bring these things to pass, Abraham decided to create an heir through one of his servants named Hagar. She gave birth to a son named Ishmael. But this was not the promised son.

Later, God granted Sarah, Abraham's wife, a son, who was named Isaac. Abraham and Isaac were the forefathers of the Jews. Abraham and Ishmael were the forefathers of the Arabs. God predicted that the Arab descendants of Ishmael would be in a continual state of hostility against their brothers the Jews.

The angel of the LORD also said to her:

"You are now with child
and you will have a son.
You shall name him Ishmael,
for the LORD has heard of your misery.
He will be a wild donkey of a man;
his hand will be against everyone
and everyone's hand against him,
and he will live in hostility
toward all his brothers."

Genesis 16:11–12

While there have been small steps toward reconciliation, the problem that began with Abraham and his two sons continues today and will continue until Jesus returns to establish his kingdom. This hatred will even intensify and become a major factor leading to the Battle of Armageddon.

2. *The Islamic Jihad.* While the nations of the Arab world continue to have their disagreements, there are three factors that unite them. One is their hatred for Israel and the Jews. Another is their language: Arabic. Third is their religion: Islam. The current growth of Islam contributes to the ongoing instability in the Middle East and the objective of driving Israel out of the land. The most dangerous element of Islam are the militant and fundamentalist groups such as Hamas and the Islamic Jihad. The feelings of militant Muslims toward Jews is no secret. It can be summarized from a sermon by Hamas leader Imam Sheik Ahmad Ibrahim at a Palestinian mosque in Gaza: "Six million descendants of

monkies [i.e., Jews] now rule all the nations of the world, but their day, too, will come. Allah, kill them all, do not leave even one."[2]

As the day of the Battle of Armageddon draws nearer, we are very likely to see a united coalition of Arab states against Israel develop. This coalition could well be driven by the passions of religious zealotry preached and practiced in the Muslim faith. Hatred driven by religious passions is the most dangerous hatred of all.

THE GEOPOLITICAL CLIMATE LEADING UP TO ARMAGEDDON

The Battle of Armageddon is the logical end of a series of events predicted in the Bible. These events shape the geographic and political scene that will exist prior to this final battle. Two of these that we have already examined are the following:

1. *Israel exists in the land.* Since the Battle of Armageddon is an attempt to eliminate the Jews and liberate Palestine from Jewish control, it is necessary that the land be under Jewish control. The Jews, having lost control of their land to the Romans in A.D. 70, regained control in 1949, when the State of Israel was established.

2. *A peace treaty guaranteed with the Antichrist.* After the rapture of the church, the world will enter the seven-year Tribulation period, during which the Antichrist will emerge as a world leader. He will bring temporary peace to the Middle East but will then break the peace treaty and eventually join the forces of Satan that gather for Armageddon.

Ed Hindson expands on these and lists ten major events that appear to be the preparation for the final battle.[3]

- Israel is back in the Promised Land for the first time in nearly two thousand years.
- The Arab nations seem bent on driving Israel into the Mediterranean Sea.
- The intervention of the major Western powers in the Middle East indicates the "times of the Gentiles" (Luke 21:24) have not ended yet.

- Attempted peace settlements, though desirable, seem destined to failure in resolving the Arab-Israeli conflict.
- Popular resentment against Israel among the Arab peoples is deeper than ever since the Gulf War of 1991.
- Iraq's attempt to rally the Arabs into a jihad ("holy war") against Israel shows how quickly an Arab coalition could form and invade Israel in the end times.
- The economic and political unification of Europe seems more probable than at any other time in recent history, possibly fulfilling Daniel's prophecies of a great end-times "revived" Roman Empire.
- The stage is now set for a prominent world leader to arise from the West, promising to bring peace to the world.
- A global economy is now upon us. It is only a matter of time until the whole world is one economic unit waiting to be taken over by a sinister power.
- The potential of nuclear war remains an ever-present reality in the world's march toward Armageddon.

A PRELUDE TO THE BATTLE

"Therefore, son of man, prophesy and say to Gog: 'This is what the Sovereign LORD says: In that day, when my people Israel are living in safety, will you not take notice of it? You will come from your place in the far north, you and many nations with you, all of them riding on horses, a great horde, a mighty army. You will advance against my people Israel like a cloud that covers the land. In days to come, O Gog, I will bring you against my land, so that the nations may know me when I show myself holy through you before their eyes.'"   *Ezekiel 38:14–16*

The prophet Ezekiel predicted an invasion of Israel by a coalition of Arab nations (Ezekiel 38–39). Scholars disagree as to when this invasion and subsequent defeat will occur. Some say these events will occur separate from and prior to the Battle of Armageddon; others regard this as a reference to Armageddon; still others interpret this as the battle that will be fought at the end of the Millennium, when Satan is released for a final battle against God. For myself, I think it is a separate battle prior to and leading to Armageddon. Several facts are predicted in regard to this invasion.

1. *The coalition forces.* The coalition will be led by "Gog, of the land of Magog, the chief prince of Meshech and Tubal" (Ezekiel 38:2). For years students of these Scriptures have identified this major coalition partner as Russia. The words "chief prince" come from the Hebrew word *rosh,* which is the root word of "Russia." The word "Meshech" is similar to Moscow, and "Tubal" is similar to Tobolsk, a large city in Russia. While these facts are certainly interesting, they are based on a questionable linguistic interpretation. We do know, however, that the land of Magog is north of Israel (v. 15). If you travel north from Palestine far enough, you will eventually reach Russia.

In light of the breakup of the Soviet Union in 1991, let me offer an alternative view on who this major partner might be. The old Soviet Union was made up of fifteen republics that now have independence. The southern republics are predominantly Muslim: Kazakhstan, Uzbekistan, Turkmenistan, Tadzhikistan, Kirgizia, and Aberbaijan. It is possible that a coalition of these Muslim countries would form the major driving force of an invasion of Israel.[4]

I have traveled in both Kazakhstan and Uzbekistan. In the latter I spent an afternoon in a local mosque talking with the mullah through an interpreter. The mullah was from Iran, a country that is exporting clergy and dollars to tighten the grip of Islam in Uzbekistan and the other new Muslim republics. With Iranian influence comes the influence of Islamic fundamentalism, which is most zealous in its hatred of and opposition to the Jews. In Uzbekistan it is illegal to convert Muslims to another faith.

The other partners in Ezekiel's predictions (vv. 5–6) are states that are now Muslim.

Persia—modern-day Iran
Cush—Sudan/Ethiopia

Put—Libya
Gomer—Cimmerians (southern Russia)
Beth Togarmah—possibly Turkey

This coalition force appears to be a jihad of Muslim countries intent on destroying Israel. Such a coalition is very possible in today's global situation.

2. *The timing of the invasion.* Several factors are mentioned in regard to the timing of this invasion. First, it will occur after Israel has been regathered to the land.

> "After many days you will be called to arms. In future years you will invade a land that has recovered from war, whose people were gathered from many nations to the mountains of Israel, which had long been desolate. They had been brought out from the nations, and now all of them live in safety."   *V. 8*

Second, it will occur when Israel exists in the land in peace and safety.

> "You will say, 'I will invade a land of unwalled villages; I will attack a peaceful and unsuspecting people—all of them living without walls and without gates and bars.'"   *V. 11*

We know from other prophetic Scriptures that the Antichrist will forge a peace treaty with Israel and guarantee its safety and security. This will occur during the first three and a half years of the Tribulation. Apart from this peace treaty, there is no other time before the coming of Jesus when Israel will exist in the land in peace and safety. Therefore it is reasonable to conclude that this invasion will take place during the first half of the Tribulation.

3. *The results of the invasion.* Ezekiel predicts a twofold outcome from the invasion by the coalition's armies. First, the invading force will be defeated. God will intervene to bring that to pass, and it will take seven months to bury the dead, presumably because of the high number of casualties of the fighting.

> "This is what will happen in that day: When Gog attacks the land of Israel, my hot anger will be aroused, declares the

Sovereign LORD. In my zeal and fiery wrath I declare that at that time there shall be a great earthquake in the land of Israel. The fish of the sea, the birds of the air, the beasts of the field, every creature that moves along the ground, and all the people on the face of the earth will tremble at my presence. The mountains will be overturned, the cliffs will crumble and every wall will fall to the ground. I will summon a sword against Gog on all my mountains, declares the Sovereign LORD. Every man's sword will be against his brother. I will execute judgment upon him with plague and bloodshed; I will pour down torrents of rain, hailstones and burning sulfur on him and on his troops and on the many nations with him."   *Ezekiel 38:18–22*

"For seven months the house of Israel will be burying them in order to cleanse the land. All the people of the land will bury them, and the day I am glorified will be a memorable day for them, declares the Sovereign LORD."
                                                        Ezekiel 39:12–13

Second, the children of Israel will begin to turn to the Lord.

"I will display my glory among the nations, and all the nations will see the punishment I inflict and the hand I lay upon them. From that day forward the house of Israel will know that I am the LORD their God."   *Ezekiel 39:21–22*

"I will no longer hide my face from them, for I will pour out my Spirit on the house of Israel, declares the Sovereign LORD."   *V. 29*

4. *The unanswered questions about the invasion.* There are several unanswered questions about this invasion. First, who will defend Israel? Some speculate that the Antichrist and his European forces will defend Israel against this attack. Some even speculate that the United States may come to Israel's defense because of its long-standing commitment to the security of Israel. But Scripture does not address this issue. A second question is, Why is the invading army led by horses—that is, cavalry? The likelihood of an invasion by cavalry seems highly unlikely, given the weapons

available for modern warfare. Some suggest that the Antichrist will bring about worldwide disarmament and that, as a result, nations will have to resort to ancient forms of warfare. Others suggest that since horses and cavalry were part of ancient warfare, the war is described in these terms because they were the tactics known to the prophet.

THE MOTHER OF ALL BATTLES

> Then they gathered the kings together to the place that in Hebrew is called Armageddon.   *Revelation 16:16*

Several smooth rocks sit on top of my desk in my office at the church. They are from Normandy beach and were given to me by a church member who stormed that beach during the Second World War. Unlike many of his fellow soldiers, he survived. I keep these rocks as a reminder of the horrors of war and the great price that was paid to liberate Europe from Nazi aggression and protect freedom. World War II was devastating in terms of its human toll. But the worst is yet to come. Armageddon will be worse than all the wars of all of time combined. A number of specific predictions are made about this battle.

1. *The opposing armies*

> The sixth angel poured out his bowl on the great river Euphrates, and its water was dried up to prepare the way for the kings from the East. Then I saw three evil spirits that looked like frogs; they came out of the mouth of the dragon, out of the mouth of the beast and out of the mouth of the false prophet. They are spirits of demons performing miraculous signs, and they go out to the kings of the whole world, to gather them for the battle on the great day of God Almighty.
> *Revelation 16:12–14*

This passage identifies the two major armies that will face each other in this last great battle. The first army is composed of "the kings from the East" and is an enormous band of 200 million (Revelation 9:16). Most people believe that the leader of this eastern coalition will be China. China has persistently maintained a large conventional army, and today it also has nuclear capabilities. It is possible that several Muslim countries from the East might join with China—Afghanistan and Pakistan, for instance—as well as other countries that have large Muslim populations, such as Malaysia, India, and Indonesia. Why would they march to the Middle East? There are two possible answers. First, this might be another Islamic jihad to exterminate the Jews. Second, the Chinese and others may want to control the oil of the Middle East, so their invasion may be motivated solely by economic factors.

The army that opposes this eastern force will be a coalition put together by the Antichrist. He will gather "the kings of the whole world" to defend Israel and repel the attack. This coalition would very likely include all the countries of the Western world: Europe, Canada, the United States, the nations of Latin America, and so on. The gathering armies will stage the ultimate conflict between East and West.

2. *A global conflict.* The major focus of the Battle of Armageddon geographically will be the land of Palestine. All the armies of the world will direct their military might toward the Middle East. But the entire world will be affected. Cities all over the world will be destroyed (Revelation 16:19). Islands and mountains will disappear (v. 20). Severe earthquakes will shake the planet (v. 18). The advancing eastern army will kill one-third of the world's population (Revelation 9:15–16). This will truly be a world war.

3. *The ultimate twist.* The Battle of Armageddon will begin with a conflict between East and West, but it will end with the East and West uniting against the armies of heaven that will accompany Jesus at his second coming.

> Then I saw the beast and the kings of the earth and their armies gathered together to make war against the rider on the horse and his army.   *Revelation 19:19*

The Bible does not indicate how the opposing armies get together to fight against Jesus. It simply states that they do and that it is the influence of Satan that draws them together (Revelation 16:14).

ALL HAIL, KING JESUS!

The battle ends with the coming of Jesus and the armies of heaven to defeat the Antichrist and his armies (Revelation 19:11–21). The entrance of Jesus onto this scene is one of the climactic moments of biblical prophecy and is described in beautiful language in the book of Revelation.

> I saw heaven standing open and there before me was a white horse, whose rider is called Faithful and True. With justice he judges and makes war. His eyes are like blazing fire, and on his head are many crowns. He has a name written on him that no one knows but he himself. He is dressed in a robe dipped in blood, and his name is the Word of God. The armies of heaven were following him, riding on white horses and dressed in fine linen, white and clean. Out of his mouth comes a sharp sword with which to strike down the nations. "He will rule them with an iron scepter." He treads the winepress of the fury of the wrath of God Almighty. On his robe and on his thigh he has this name written:
>
> KING OF KINGS AND LORD OF LORDS.
>
> *Revelation 19:11–16*

Chapter 9

THE MILLENNIUM

Joy to the world! the Lord is come!
Let earth receive her King;
Let ev'ry heart prepare Him room,
And heav'n and nature sing.

Earlier in the book we recited the hymn "Joy to the World"—
a hymn, not about Christmas, but about the second coming of
Christ. The words are based on Psalm 98 and speak of Jesus' coming to earth as the King, of his worldwide rule, and of the restraining of nature and the reversing of the curse. These are all
descriptive of the Second Coming, when Jesus will establish the
millennial kingdom—a reign of a thousand years.

THE SECOND COMING OF JESUS

When Jesus entered the world the first time, he did it quietly
and in relative obscurity. As God taking human form, he was born
in Bethlehem, and his mother wrapped him in swaddling clothes

and placed him in a manger (Luke 2:7). For thirty years he lived in Nazareth in the home of a carpenter. After three years of public ministry he was crucified, was buried in a tomb, and was resurrected three days later. Forty days after that, he returned to heaven. Apart from those who knew him in the land of Palestine, all this passed without notice by the larger world. But Jesus' second coming will be vastly different from the first. He will not tiptoe into the world. Rather, he will come with power, glory, and the armies of heaven.

> *Look, he is coming with the clouds,*
>   *and every eye will see him,*
> *even those who pierced him;*
>   *and all the peoples of the earth will mourn because of him.*
>   *So shall it be! Amen.*
>
> *Revelation 1:7*

The attention of the entire world will be focused on this dramatic event. In his book *The King Is Coming*, Harold Willmington contrasts the first coming of Jesus—his suffering—with the second coming—his glory.[1]

a. *The sufferings*—A Baby, wrapped in swaddling clothes (Luke 2:12).
   The glory—A King, clothed in majestic apparel (Psa. 93:1).

b. *The sufferings*—He was the wearied traveler (John 4:6).
   The glory—He will be the untiring God (Isa. 40:28, 29).

c. *The sufferings*—He had nowhere to lay his head (Luke 9:58).
   The glory—He will become heir to all things (Heb. 1:2).

d. *The sufferings*—He was rejected by tiny Israel (John 1:11).
   The glory—He will be accepted by all the nations (Isa. 9:6).

e. *The sufferings*—Wicked men took up stones to throw at him (John 8:59).
The glory—Wicked men will cry for stones to fall upon them to hide them from him (Rev. 6:16).

f. *The sufferings*—A lowly Savior, acquainted with grief (Isa. 53:3).
The glory—The mighty God, anointed with the oil of gladness (Heb. 1:9).

g. *The sufferings*—He was clothed with a scarlet robe in mockery (Luke 23:11).
The glory—He will be clothed with a vesture dipped in the blood of his enemies (Rev. 19:13).

h. *The sufferings*—He was smitten with a reed (Matt. 27:30).
The glory—He will rule the nations with a rod of iron (Rev. 19:15).

i. *The sufferings*—Wicked soldiers bowed their knee and mocked (Mark 15:19).
The glory—Every knee shall bow and acknowledge Him (Phil. 2:10).

j. *The sufferings*—He wore the crown of thorns (John 19:5).
The glory—He will wear the crown of gold (Rev. 14:14).

k. *The sufferings*—His hands were pierced with nails (John 20:25).
The glory—His hands will carry a sharp sickle (Rev. 14:14).

l. *The sufferings*—His feet were pierced with nails (Psa. 22:16).
The glory—His feet will stand on the Mount of Olives (Zech. 14:4).

m. *The sufferings*—He had no form or comeliness
(Isa. 53:2).
The glory—He will be the fairest of ten thousand
(Psa. 27:4).

n. *The sufferings*—He delivered up his spirit (John 19:30).
The glory—He is alive forevermore (Rev. 1:18).

o. *The sufferings*—He was laid in the tomb
(Matt. 27:59, 60).
The glory—He will sit on his throne (Heb. 8:1).

The next major prophetic event in God's timetable is the rapture of the church. At that time, God will take all believers to heaven. After that, the seven-year Tribulation will begin, which will see the rise of the Antichrist and will conclude with the Battle of Armageddon.

In that battle, as we have seen, Jesus will come again to the earth to lead the armies that will fight against the forces of Satan.

> A day of the LORD is coming when your plunder will be
> divided among you. I will gather all the nations to Jerusalem
> to fight against it; the city will be captured, the houses ransacked, and the women raped. Half of the city will go into
> exile, but the rest of the people will not be taken from the city.
> Then the LORD will go out and fight against those nations, as
> he fights in the day of battle.   *Zechariah 14:1–3*

The Bible describes what Jesus will do when he returns.

1. *The armies of the world will gather to fight against Israel and Jerusalem*. The gathering of the world's armies to the Battle of Armageddon is the event that will trigger the second coming of Jesus Christ. During this battle, Jerusalem will be captured and ransacked (Zechariah 14:1–2).

2. *Jesus will descend and stand on the Mount of Olives* (vv. 3–5). When Jesus went back to heaven (Acts 2), he did so from the Mount of Olives. When he returns to earth, he will arrive at the same place whence he departed. The mountain will be split in two by a great earthquake; the split will run east to the Dead Sea and west to

the Mediterranean. In his best-selling book *The Late Great Planet Earth*, Hal Lindsey reports that "an oil company doing seismic studies of this area in quest of oil discovered a gigantic fault running east and west precisely through the center of the Mount of Olives."[2]

3. *Jesus will come with the saints and the armies of heaven* (v. 5). Jesus will not return alone to the Mount of Olives. He will come with "all the holy ones"—most likely a reference to the angelic armies of heaven and the believers who are already in the presence of God (Revelation 19:14).

4. *Jesus will defeat the armies who are fighting against Jerusalem* (Zechariah 14:12–13). The enemy armies will be struck with a plague, and their flesh will rot—along with their eyes and tongues. This will cause confusion, and the soldiers will actually begin to fight each other.

5. *Jesus will establish his kingdom over the entire world* (v. 9). This will mark the beginning of the millennial kingdom, the thousand-year reign of Jesus on the earth (Revelation 20:4–6). The kingdom will have its headquarters in Jerusalem, and that city will become the center of the worship of Jesus Christ (Zechariah 14:16–19).

> This is what the LORD Almighty says: "Many peoples and the inhabitants of many cities will yet come, and the inhabitants of one city will go to another and say, 'Let us go at once to entreat the LORD and seek the LORD Almighty. I myself am going.' And many peoples and powerful nations will come to Jerusalem to seek the LORD Almighty and to entreat him."
>
> This is what the LORD Almighty says: "In those days ten men from all languages and nations will take firm hold of one Jew by the hem of his robe and say, 'Let us go with you, because we have heard that God is with you.'"
>
> *Zechariah 8:20–23*

THE MILLENNIAL KINGDOM

The Bible has much to say about the millennial kingdom of Christ.

1. *Satan will be removed from the earth.*

> And I saw an angel coming down out of heaven, having
> the key to the Abyss and holding in his hand a great chain.
> He seized the dragon, that ancient serpent, who is the devil,
> or Satan, and bound him for a thousand years. He threw him
> into the Abyss, and locked and sealed it over him, to keep
> him from deceiving the nations anymore until the thousand
> years were ended. After that, he must be set free for a short
> time.   *Revelation 20:1–3*

The thousand-year reign will be free of the influence and
work of Satan. The history of the human race is one of a continual battle between good and evil, Satan and God. During the Millennium this archenemy of God will be removed from the earth.
This does not mean that everyone on the earth will then accept
Jesus. In fact, after the Millennium Satan is unbound for a short
period of time and he gathers a worldwide army for one final battle with God (vv. 7–10).

2. *All of Israel will be saved.* The Bible describes our age of
history as "the times of the Gentiles." During this time Israel has
hardened her heart against God. But when Jesus returns to establish his kingdom, all of Israel will be saved (Romans 11:25–27).
Israel will have a place of prominence among the nations of the
world (Isaiah 14:1–2). All nations will bow in submission to Israel
(Isaiah 49:22–23).

3. *It will be a time of peace.*

> *For to us a child is born,*
> > *to us a son is given,*
> > *and the government will be on his shoulders.*
> *And he will be called*
> > *Wonderful Counselor, Mighty God,*
> > *Everlasting Father, Prince of Peace.*
> *Of the increase of his government and peace*
> > *there will be no end.*
> *He will reign on David's throne*
> > *and over his kingdom,*
> *establishing and upholding it*

> *with justice and righteousness*
> *from that time on and forever.*
> *The zeal of the LORD Almighty*
> *will accomplish this.*
>
> *Isaiah 9:6–7*

As the "Prince of Peace," Jesus will bring never-ending peace to the world. This peace includes the cessation of war and a time of global economic prosperity. Both these conditions are major themes of the Old Testament prophets. During this time nations will "beat their swords into plowshares and their spears into pruning hooks. Nation will not take up sword against nation, nor will they train for war anymore" (Isaiah 2:4). Even the hostile relationships in the natural order will cease: "The wolf will live with the lamb. . . . The cow will feed with the bear. . . . The infant will play near the hole of the cobra" (Isaiah 11:6–8). Peace will extend to individual communities: "My people will live in peaceful dwelling places, in secure homes, in undisturbed places of rest" (Isaiah 32:18). Tyranny and terror will no longer be feared (Isaiah 54:14). Creation will be renewed and restored, and "the mountains and hills will burst into song" (Isaiah 55:12).

The millennial peacetime will also see economic prosperity (Ezekiel 28:25–26). The prophet Micah captures the essence and spirit of the millennial kingdom.

> Many nations will come and say,
>
> *"Come, let us go up to the mountain of the LORD,*
> *to the house of the God of Jacob.*
> *He will teach us his ways,*
> *so that we may walk in his paths."*
> *The law will go out from Zion,*
> *the word of the LORD from Jerusalem.*
> *He will judge between many peoples*
> *and will settle disputes for strong nations far and wide. . . .*
> *Every man will sit under his own vine*
> *and under his own fig tree,*
> *and no one will make them afraid,*
> *for the LORD Almighty has spoken.*
>
> *Micah 4:2–4*

4. *Jesus will rule the world from Jerusalem.*

"In my vision at night I looked, and there before me was one like a son of man, coming with the clouds of heaven. He approached the Ancient of Days and was led into his presence. He was given authority, glory and sovereign power; all peoples, nations and men of every language worshiped him. His dominion is an everlasting dominion that will not pass away, and his kingdom is one that will never be destroyed."

Daniel 7:13–14

One of the most elaborate descriptions of the future kingdom is found in Isaiah 11. Isaiah predicts that the future king will be a descendant of Jesse, who was the father of King David (v. 1). The king will have the spirit of wisdom, understanding, counsel, power, knowledge, and fear (v. 2). He will judge the nations of the world (v. 3). He will establish justice and righteousness and defend the poor and needy (v. 4). He will remove the hostility in nature that was the result of sin (vv. 6–9). All the nations of the world will submit to him (v. 10).

5. *There will be economic prosperity.* During the Tribulation the earth will be devastated by wars—possibly nuclear war—and natural disasters, famines, and disease. During the millennial kingdom the earth will be restored, and people will enjoy unparalleled economic prosperity. Land that showed no potential for agriculture will be transformed: "the wilderness will rejoice and blossom" (Isaiah 35:1). During the Tribulation the rivers, lakes, and seas will become polluted and poisoned, but during the Millennium, "the burning sand will become a pool, the thirsty ground bubbling springs" (v. 7). The elements necessary for a rich harvest will be restored (Isaiah 30:23), and there will be extended warmth and light to enhance the quality of life on the earth (v. 26).

The prophet Amos describes this new world order and its economic prosperity this way:

"The days are coming," declares the LORD,
"when the reaper will be overtaken by the plowman
*   and the planter by the one treading grapes.*

New wine will drip from the mountains
   and flow from all the hills.
I will bring back my exiled people Israel;
   they will rebuild the ruined cities and live in them.
They will plant vineyards and drink their wine;
   they will make gardens and eat their fruit.
I will plant Israel in their own land,
   never again to be uprooted
   from the land I have given them,"
      says the LORD your God.

                                                    Amos 9:13–15

6. *Jerusalem will be the center of worship.* Jerusalem will be the capital city of the millennial kingdom as well as its economic, judicial, and religious center. The temple will be the focal point of worship. The details of this temple and its worship are outlined in the prophecy of Ezekiel 40–48. Although this kingdom temple will be similar in some ways to the temples of Solomon and Herod, it will also be different. For example, there will be no veil, or curtain, separating the Holy Place from the Most Holy Place (2 Chronicles 3:14). Nor will there be a golden table for the bread of the Presence (2 Chronicles 4:19) or golden lampstands (v. 20) or the ark of the covenant (2 Chronicles 5:7). The reason is that Jesus split the curtain in two (Matthew 27:51), and he is both the bread of life (John 6:35) and the light of the world (John 8:12).

Regular sacrifices will be made at the brazen altar in the temple.

"All Kedar's flocks will be gathered to you,
   the rams of Nebaioth will serve you;
they will be accepted as offerings on my altar,
   and I will adorn my glorious temple."

                                                    Isaiah 60:7
                                       (see also Isaiah 56:4–8)

The issue of animal sacrifices raises an important theological question. Why will the sacrifices be offered when they have no redemptive value? When Jesus died, he offered himself as a sacrifice "once for all" (Hebrews 10:10). The Bible makes it clear that Old Testament sacrifices were only a "shadow" and could not take away sin. They pointed to the only sacrifice that can remove sin: the sacrifice of Jesus Christ. So why would these sacrifices be restored during the millennial kingdom? Harold Willmington suggests four possible reasons.

    a. A reminder to all of the necessity of the new birth.

    b. An object lesson of the costliness of salvation.

    c. An example of the awfulness of sin.

    d. An illustration of the holiness of God.[3]

In the Old Testament the sacrifices pointed *forward* to the Cross. In the millennial kingdom the sacrifices point *back* toward the Cross.

7. *The worldwide government of Jesus will be administered by his followers.* Jesus promised his twelve disciples that when he "sits on his glorious throne" they would also "sit on twelve thrones, judging the twelve tribes of Israel" (Matthew 19:28). Likewise, he promised rewards and blessings for everyone who had followed him (v. 29). We know that in the future kingdom, we believers will judge the world (1 Corinthians 6:2); the saints will judge and rule over the earth as an extension of Jesus' authority. The twelve disciples will have the most prominent positions of power and influence in the government of Jesus.

THE FINAL CONFLICT AND THE FINAL STATE

At the end of the millennial kingdom, Satan will be released from the Abyss and undertake one final revolt against God. He will deceive the nations and gather them for battle against Jesus and his kingdom. The armies of Satan will surround Jerusalem, but they will be destroyed by fire from heaven. Satan will then be thrown into the lake of fire (Revelation 20:11–15).

A "new heaven and a new earth" will come into existence to replace the old heaven and the old earth. The language that describes this new creation is some of the most beautiful in all of Scripture.

> I saw the Holy City, the new Jerusalem, coming down out of heaven from God, prepared as a bride beautifully dressed for her husband. And I heard a loud voice from the throne saying, "Now the dwelling of God is with men, and he will live with them. They will be his people, and God himself will be with them and be their God. He will wipe every tear from their eyes. There will be no more death or mourning or crying or pain, for the old order of things has passed away."
>
> He who was seated on the throne said, "I am making everything new!" Then he said, "Write this down, for these words are trustworthy and true."   *Revelation 21:2–5*

Chapter 10

FIFTY REMARKABLE EVENTS POINTING TOWARD THE END

Since Jesus returned to heaven, nearly every generation of Bible students and scholars has interpreted biblical prophecy through the filter of its own historical experience. Many have concluded that they were living in the last days and that the events around them were the direct fulfillment of biblical prophecy. We saw in chapter 5 that Martin Luther identified the pope with the Antichrist. The Puritans also saw the pope as the Antichrist and the "locusts from the bottomless pit as his agents: monks, friars, cardinals, patriarchs, and bishops."[1] In more recent times various people have been identified as the Antichrist, including Kaiser Wilhelm, Benito Mussolini, Adolf Hitler, Joseph Stalin, Nikita Khrushchev, and Saddam Hussein.[2]

I remember that in the fall of 1988 the evangelical Christian community was captivated by a booklet entitled *88 Reasons Why the Rapture Will Be in 1988*.[3] This booklet contained a complicated analysis of Rosh Hashanah (the Jewish Feast of Trumpets), which is often associated with the rapture of the church because of the presence of trumpets in both events. The writer calculated that the exact date of the Rapture would be September 12, 1988. As the date approached, it was hard to find any of the booklets in stores because they were in such high demand. Religious and secular media covered the story. But the writer was wrong! I have a copy of the booklet in my office, and it's hardly worth giving or throwing away. The irony of this is that every person who has identified biblical events with current events to conclude that we were living in the last days has been wrong! So why does this book have a chapter entitled "Fifty Remarkable Events Pointing Toward the End"?

I am fully aware that I may be falling into the same trap as generations of Bible expositors who have preceded me. But I base this chapter on three facts. First, the Bible makes detailed predictions about the global situation as we approach the end of the age. Second, many current events bear a remarkable similarity to these detailed predictions of Scripture. Third, each of us will have to judge for oneself whether it is likely or not that we are living in the last days. I believe that no single event would lead us to the conclusion that the end is near but that the cumulative impact of all these predictions and events causes one to wonder. For clarity, I have divided the predictions and events into several major categories and have numbered them. Most of the predictions and events have been dealt with in detail in previous chapters, so in what follows I make only a brief statement about them.

POLITICAL PREDICTIONS AND EVENTS

The Bible describes the geopolitical situation that will prevail as we approach the end of the world.

#1. *The return of the Jewish people to Israel.* The focus of international attention in the end times will be the nation of Israel. The Bible predicts the regathering of Jews back to the land (Ezekiel 37). The events foretold for the Tribulation, the Battle of Armageddon, and the millennial kingdom all require that Israel be constituted a nation in the land of Palestine. In the twentieth century, for the first time since Jesus returned to heaven, Israel exists as a nation and the Jews are returning to the land.

#2. *Jerusalem under Jewish control.* Although the State of Israel was established on May 14, 1948, the city of Jerusalem did not come under Jewish control at that time. Many prophecies about end times deal with Jerusalem, and they all assume that the city is under Jewish control. Jerusalem was destroyed by the Romans in A.D. 70, and the Jews never regained possession of the city until the Six-Day War of 1967.

#3. *The times of the Gentiles coming to an end.* The current age is known biblically as "the times of the Gentiles." God's primary, but not exclusive, focus lies with the Gentiles. Israel has hardened its heart during this time period (Romans 10:25), but once the gentile age is over, God will renew his favor toward Israel and the Jewish people. Jesus predicted that "Jerusalem will be trampled on by the Gentiles until the times of the Gentiles are fulfilled" (Luke 21:24). Until 1967, Jerusalem was "trampled on" by the Gentiles. But no longer. This could mean that we are in the last of the last days of the Gentiles.

#4. *The nation of Israel born in a day.* In regard to the regathering of the Jews to Israel, the Bible predicts that the nation would be born in one day.

> *"Who has ever heard of such a thing?*
>   *Who has ever seen such things?*
> *Can a country be born in a day*
>   *or a nation be brought forth in a moment?*
> *Yet no sooner is Zion in labor*
>   *than she gives birth to her children."*
>
>   *Isaiah 66:8*

On May 14, 1948, David Ben-Gurion, who would become the prime minister, read the Scroll of Independence in the Tel Aviv Museum. "By virtue of our national and intrinsic right and on the strength of the resolution of the United Nations General Assembly, we hereby declare the establishment of a Jewish State of Palestine, which shall be known as the State of Israel." Israel was born in a day.

#5. *The formation of the State of Israel as the ultimate sign of the end of the age*. When Jesus addressed the signs of his second coming and the end of the age, he warned his disciples to "learn this lesson from the fig tree: As soon as its twigs get tender and its leaves come out, you know that summer is near" (Matthew 24:32). Many Bible scholars believe that the fig tree refers to the State of Israel—a recurring image in Scripture. If that is so, then the blossoming of the fig tree—that is, the regathering of the Jews to Israel—will signal that the end is near.

#6. *Ongoing hostility between Israel and its neighbors*. During the Tribulation there will be two major attempts to invade Israel. The first will be led by a northern power and the second by an eastern power (see #8 and #9). Both armies will be drawn from a coalition of nations that are bent on the destruction of Israel. The current geopolitical situation in the Middle East makes this possible.

#7. *Ongoing attempts at peace in the Middle East*. The Bible predicts that the Antichrist will forge a peace treaty with Israel that will guarantee its security. He will gain global prominence because of his ability to bring peace to the Middle East when so many others have tried and failed. The current relationship between the Jews and the Palestinians is at best a fragile peace, as the assassination of Israeli prime minister Yitzhak Rabin reveals.

#8. *The development of a northern coalition army that will invade Israel*. The prophet Ezekiel predicted the invasion of Israel by a coalition army led by a powerful northern land called Gog. This could be a northern coalition of Muslim countries such as Kazakhstan, Uzbekistan, Turkmenistan, Tadzhikistan, Kirgizia, and Aberbaijan—all formerly part of the Soviet Union. Countries joining with them could be Iran, Sudan, Ethiopia, and Libya—all having strong Muslim influence. It appears that this invasion will be driven by Muslim passion. The current political situation makes such a coalition possible.

#9. *The rise of a massive army in the East*. The major army that invades Israel for the Battle of Armageddon is a massive army from the East. The Bible predicts that the army will be 200 million strong—an incredible number of people. China, a nation with more than a billion people, maintains the largest conventional army in the world and has nuclear capabilities.

#10. *The revival of the ancient Roman Empire.* The prophet Daniel predicted that the Roman Empire would exist in two phases. The first phase would follow the Greek Empire; the second would emerge prior to the coming of Jesus and the end of the world. The second phase would take the form of a political coalition of separate nations covering basically the same geography as the original Roman Empire. The current push for unity through the European Economic Community offers a very close parallel to the biblical prediction.

#11. *The fall of the Berlin wall as a prelude to the revived Roman Empire.* Since World War II, Europe has been divided between East and West. Given the power and control of communism over the Eastern bloc countries, few expected the wall to fall and East and West to be united. But much to the amazement of the world, the wall of communism fell and now all Europe is opened to the possibility of political and economic unity.

#12. *Europe becoming the economic and military leader of the world.* The Bible predicts that the Antichrist will rise to world power out of a European coalition. This coalition and its armies will be the defenders of Israel in the initial stages of the Battle of Armageddon. As the world turns increasingly to the Antichrist for leadership, Europe will take the center stage.

#13. *A major shift toward globalism.* The Bible predicts that at the end of the world there will be a one-world government, economy, and church. A hundred years ago such talk would have been ridiculed. Technology and travel were the major obstacles to worldwide cooperation. But with faxes, computers, telephones, e-mail, and airplanes, the world has become a global village.

#14. *The United Nations as a model for the future.* As we approach the end of the world, affairs will become oriented toward the international community and the good of the entire globe—not just an individual nation. During the Tribulation, the Antichrist will be the major power that influences and governs the entire world. The United Nations currently exists as a model of what the Bible predicts will happen in regard to one-world government. More and more, the U.N. is imposing its will on the international community; even American troops are serving under U.N. authority.

#15. *Increased international instability*. Jesus predicted that as we approach the end of the age there would be "wars and rumors of wars" (Matthew 24:6). The increased instability of the world will give rise to the need for international cooperation. It will also set the stage for the rise of a skilled negotiator who can forge peace around the world—namely, the Antichrist.

#16. *The emergence of the Antichrist*. The Bible predicts that the Antichrist will emerge as the leader of the world. As a skilled negotiator who will forge international peace, he will dominate the world. Given the many conflicts going on around the world, we can see why many people will look for a "superhuman" diplomat who can begin to restore order on a grand scale.

#17. *The introduction of new paradigms in the New World Order*. When the Antichrist comes to power, he will realign national boundaries and redistribute material resources. He will also change long-standing national and moral laws (Daniel 7:25). He will introduce new paradigms that will regulate life under his regime. I believe that, given the instability of the world and the complex problems we face, the world will be open to the new paradigms offered by the Antichrist.

#18. *A one-world economy*. Along with the shift toward a one-world government will come a shift toward a one-world economy. This economy will be controlled entirely by the Antichrist. Trading will only be allowed for those who have the mark of the Beast: 666. We are already well on the way toward a one-world economy.

#19. *The threat of nuclear extinction*. The threat of nuclear war is the ongoing dilemma in the world today. We have the potential to destroy most of the world as we know it just by pushing a button. During the Tribulation there will be massive destruction of people and the environment. The descriptions of these disasters (as in 2 Peter 3:10) have striking similarities to the consequences of nuclear war.

TECHNOLOGICAL PREDICTIONS AND EVENTS

#20. *The increase of knowledge*. Centuries ago, God gave the prophet Daniel specific instructions: "But you, Daniel, close up and seal the words of the scroll until the time of the end. Many will go here and there to increase knowledge" (Daniel 12:4). This seems to indicate an explosion of knowledge and the pursuit of knowledge at the end of the world. We now live along the "information superhighway," and knowledge has increased exponentially in our generation.

#21. *A move toward a cashless society*. During the Tribulation, when the Antichrist is in power, only people who possess the mark of the Beast can do business. It appears that business will be conducted without cash. This is already the trend in our own country and many other nations.

#22. *The advent of television*. During the Tribulation miraculous events will transpire that will be watched by the whole world at the same time (Revelation 13:13). Before the advent of television, people predicted that the events would be supernaturally imposed in the sky so all people could see them. However, television has changed all that; CNN has changed the way we watch news events. Now we can watch events live from anywhere in the world.

#23. *The advent of computers*. During the Tribulation it will be necessary to have the mark of the Beast (666) in order to buy and sell. This mark would be on the right hand or forehead. The computer technology already exists to accomplish this.

RELIGIOUS PREDICTIONS AND EVENTS

#24. *The rebuilding of the temple in Jerusalem*. The temple in Jerusalem will be partially or fully rebuilt for the Tribulation period. There is passionate interest among many Jews in rebuilding the temple even though the Dome of the Rock, a sacred Muslim site, stands in the way. The Temple Institute, for example, has already made more than a hundred of the utensils needed for temple worship; they are on display at the Temple Institute Tourist Center.[4]

#25. *The reestablishment of the priesthood.* The Bible predicts that the sons of Zadok will perform religious duties as priests in the rebuilt temple (Ezekiel 40:46). The Ateret Cohanim is a religious school in Israel that is now training temple priests for future service when the temple is rebuilt and worship is restored.[5]

#26. *The return to animal sacrifices and temple festivities.* During the Tribulation and the Millennium, offerings and religious activities will take place at the rebuilt temple in Jerusalem. Preparations are already under way to facilitate these religious practices and duties. "Clothing is being made, harps constructed, computer-designed architectural plans made, and some rabbis are deciding what modern innovations can be adopted into a new temple. Also, an effort is well under way to secure Kosher animals for sacrifice, including red heifers."[6]

#27. *A shift toward one-world religion.* The Bible predicts that during the Tribulation a one-world religion will emerge alongside a one-world government and a one-world economy. Of all the end-time predictions, this is the most difficult to understand because the current world is so divided over religion and religious beliefs. A one-world religion is hard to imagine. Perhaps it will not be a single religion, but rather a level of cooperation among all the major religions of the world to advance the global government and global economy.

#28. *The rise of Islam.* The rise of Islam is not specifically predicted in any prophetic passages of the Bible. However, many of the nations that will form a coalition to invade Israel are both Arab and Muslim. The rising influence of Islam and its hatred toward the Jews and Israel will continue to fuel animosity and very likely pave the way for massive attacks to exterminate the Jews and their nation.

#29. *The gospel preached in all the world.* Jesus predicted that "this gospel of the kingdom will be preached in the whole world as a testimony to all nations, and then the end will come"

(Matthew 24:14). Today there is a concerted effort among evangelical Christians, churches, and missions organizations to get the gospel to every person on the globe by the year 2000. It is called the A.D. 2000 Movement, and its goal is the gospel for every person and a church for every people group. We now have the technology, resources, strategies, and cooperation needed to accomplish this mission. Could the coming of Jesus be far behind?

JESUS AND THE SIGNS OF THE END OF THE WORLD

Jesus told his disciples what would happen as we approach the end of the world.

#30. *False messiahs* (Matthew 24:24). Jesus predicted that many would come in his name claiming to be the Christ, or messiah. This is confirmed in other Bible passages. We are warned against false teachers (2 Peter 2:1–3) and false apostles (2 Corinthians 11:13–14). Jesus even predicted that these false Christs and false prophets would "perform great signs and miracles" (Matthew 24:24).

#31. *Wars and rumors of wars* (vv. 6–7). As we approach the end, the world will not get better; it will get worse. Jesus said, "Nation will rise against nation, and kingdom against kingdom." While people will seek peace, they will only experience war. According to the United Nations, the three largest industries in the world are

> The military—800 billion dollars a year
> Illegal drugs—500 billion dollars a year
> Oil—450 billion dollars a year[7]

Is it any wonder that the world is very unstable with continuing conflicts and hostilities?

#32. *Famines* (v. 7). In addition to the predictions of Jesus, other Bible passages predict worldwide famine during the Tribulation (for example, Revelation 6:6). Scientists are most concerned about the growth in the world's population and humanity's inability to grow enough food to feed itself. Global famine is a realistic possibility.

#33. *Earthquakes* (Matthew 24:7). Most students of prophecy claim that in recent years the number of earthquakes has increased. However, this is not true, according to the National Earthquake Information Center, which says that the number of earthquakes of 7.0 magnitude or greater has remained the same throughout this century. But earthquakes continue, and the United States is perpetually on the lookout for "the Big One" in California.

#34. *The persecution of Christians* (v. 9). The world has always hated Christians—even as it hated Jesus. But as the spirit of the age becomes increasingly that of Antichrist, there will be more persecution of Christians. Christians will even be martyred for their faith—a trend that becomes more evident day by day around the world.

#35. *An increase of wickedness* (v. 12). As the end approaches, so will the increase of wickedness and sin. In spite of the world's advances in science, technology, and medicine, the world will become worse instead of better. The apostle Paul confirms this trend (2 Timothy 3:1–9) and describes the cultural climate of the last days as "terrible times" (v. 1).

#36. *The darkening of the sun and the moon* (Matthew 24:29). One aftermath of a nuclear explosion is what scientists call "twilight at noon." The air becomes filled with particle matter that is light absorbing and reflecting. As a result, the light of the sun and moon become obscured. Could this be what Jesus predicted?

#37. *Cataclysmic events in the universe* (v. 29). Jesus predicted that "the stars will fall from the sky, and the heavenly bodies will be shaken." This prediction is confirmed by events foretold in Revelation 6:12–14. During the Tribulation, in the days preceding the second coming of Jesus, the universe begins to shake and crumble. Current concern about an asteroid hitting the earth parallels these biblical predictions.

#38. *Widespread disregard for the signs of Jesus' coming* (Matthew 24:37–39). In the days of Noah, people went about their business and paid no attention to his warnings of impending judgment. Jesus predicted that the same would be true in the last days: warnings about the Second Coming will be ignored. Life will go on as usual with no regard for God. In fact, those who speak of the second coming of Jesus will be labeled "anti-intellectual."

ENVIRONMENTAL PREDICTIONS AND EVENTS

#39. *The pollution of the seas* (Revelation 8:8). During the Tribulation one-third of the oceans will become polluted. This pollution will cause the death of one-third of the creatures who live in the sea. There is already global concern about our abuse and misuse of the oceans. The problem will reach immense proportions during the Tribulation.

#40. *The pollution of rivers and drinking water* (vv. 10–11). One-third of the waters and rivers will become polluted and poisoned during the Tribulation. People will die as a result of drinking this polluted water.

#41. *The destruction of forests and grasslands* (v. 7). During the Tribulation one-third of the land on the earth will be burned up. One-third of the forests and all the green grass will be consumed by fire. Could this be the aftermath of a nuclear explosion? The result will be massive changes in the climate and the quality of life for human beings.

#42. *Uncontrolled diseases and plagues that kill more than one-fourth of the earth's population* (Revelation 6:8). We live in the most medically and technically advanced time in human history. We have modern hospitals, well-trained doctors, and equipment and medicines such as have never been known before. Yet the Bible predicts that during the Tribulation diseases will run unchecked and millions will die. Our inability to cure HIV and AIDS will be multiplied over and over with other diseases and plagues.

#43. *A general environment that is not friendly to life.* When we consider the pollution and other physical devastation predicted for the Tribulation along with the specter of widespread famine and epidemics, one thing is certain: the environment at the end of the world will be most hostile toward sustaining life. In fact, life will become miserable. People will curse God and want to die (Revelation 16:9, 11).

CULTURAL PREDICTIONS AND EVENTS

In describing the last days as "terrible times" (2 Timothy 3:1), the apostle Paul lists nineteen characteristics of society and cultures for those times. I have grouped these characteristics into seven categories.

#44. *People in love with themselves* (v. 2). As the first characteristic that Paul lists, this seems to be the predominant trait of people in the last days. The current New Age phenomena and the self-help movement both have a premise of self-love. "Get in touch with the god you are," New Age gurus state. "Whatever your problem, you can resolve it. You are somebody. Love yourself." Self-help advocates peddle the same idea. Both these ideologies are deeply rooted in Western culture.

#45. *Materialism* (v. 2). Paul describes materialistic people as "lovers of money." Loving money is really an extension of loving self. The pursuit of money is generally for self-gratification. Again, Western culture is propped up on the pillars of money and things.

#46. *Narcissism* (vv. 3–4). Another characteristic of people at the end of the world is unrestrained hedonism and narcissism. They will be "lovers of pleasure more than lovers of God."

#47. *Arrogance* (vv. 1–5). Paul uses several words to describe the human arrogance that will be prevalent in the last days: "boastful, proud, . . . rash, conceited."

#48. *Abusive* (vv. 2–4). Abusive language and actions go along with arrogance and self-centeredness. Paul calls the guilty ones "abusive," "slanderous," "brutal," and "treacherous."

#49. *Broken family and personal relationships* (vv. 1–5). The net result of self-love is the inevitable breakdown of family and personal relationships. Paul states that people will be "disobedient to their parents, ungrateful, . . . without love, unforgiving." Family ties will be severed. People will become increasingly alienated from each other and incapable of restoring their broken relationships.

#50. *People living without self-control* (vv. 2–4). Perhaps the most dangerous trait of people in the last days is the lack of self-control. They will not love good, but will live unholy and uncontrolled lives. This will lead to the breakdown of an ordered and structured society. People won't care anymore. They will do as they please. The result will be worldwide chaos and anarchy. This is precisely the kind of global situation that will give rise to a world dictator—the Antichrist—who promises to bring order and structure to a world falling apart.

SUMMARY

What does the Bible predict about the end of the world? I have just listed fifty specific predictions that have remarkable similarity to the world in which we live. Taken individually or in small groups, the predictions are interesting, but not necessarily compelling. But when you read all of them, you cannot help but wonder if we are not *now* living in the last days.

As I write this chapter, I am at home alone. My wife and children are skiing in northern Michigan. Toward the end of the chapter I was overcome with the deep sensation that Jesus could come at any moment. At no other time in human history since Jesus ascended to heaven have so many incredible prophetic events come together. As I wrote, I could feel my heart begin to beat faster. I thought, "Jesus could come today!" For a moment I thought of getting into the car and driving to meet my family so that I could be with them if Jesus came. But then I realized that if he did come, we would meet together in the air (1 Thessalonians 4:13–18).

Chapter 11

TOP TEN LIST OF MOST FREQUENTLY ASKED QUESTIONS ABOUT THE END TIMES

Over the years, as I have preached and taught biblical eschatology—the theology of "last things"—I have tended to hear some questions over and over again. Usually people ask these questions in response to a sermon or a book or a radio or television program. I have made a list of those most frequently asked. While it was not compiled scientifically, I think the list is fairly representative of what is on the mind of most people who are interested in end-time prophecies.

WHAT IS THE ROLE OF THE UNITED STATES IN BIBLE PROPHECY?

This is by far the most frequently asked question, yet I find it a strange one. I grew up in Belfast, Northern Ireland. I attended many prophecy conferences there and do not recall hearing anyone talk about the role of the United States. We were interested in Great Britain and its relationship to the European community. We saw ourselves as part of the revived Roman Empire predicted in Scripture. For us, the United States was not important. But when I came to this country I discovered that nearly everyone is interested in how the United States fits into end-time prophecies.

There is a sense in which this question is somewhat self-serving. After all, why are people not asking about the role of Brazil or Australia or India or Argentina? Do these nations not matter as much as the United States? Although the question is somewhat arrogant, it is nevertheless important because the United States is the leading superpower in the world at this time.

So what is the role of the United States in prophecies about the end of the world? The United States is not mentioned directly, of course, any more than Great Britain or Germany or China is. This seems actually quite remarkable. If we are living in the last days, would it not be important to identify the role of the most powerful nation in the world? Over the years scholars have struggled to answer this question. There are at least three options in regard to the United States and biblical prophecies.

First, some propose that the United States is included symbolically in the revived Roman Empire. Since the United States was founded by European immigrants and has strong European roots, it is in fact a cultural extension of the European community. As the end of the world approaches, the United States will continue its military, economic, and political cooperation with Europe.

Second, other people suggest that as we approach the end of the world, the United States will deteriorate and decline and lose its influence internationally as a superpower. Jack Van Impe makes a compelling case for this viewpoint in his book *2001: On the Edge of Eternity*. He lists the extensive moral, social, spiritual, and cultural problems that are on the rise in the United States. He then asks the questions, "Can America survive this moral decline?" and "Are we not facing the judgment of God?" He suggests that there may be veiled references to the United States in Isaiah 18:1–2;

Jeremiah 50–51; and Ezekiel 38:13. Each of these passages foretells the judgment of God on specific nations—one of which, he argues, may allude to the United States.[1] Thus the nation will be reduced to international insignificance by the judgment of God.

Third, I believe, with others, that the United States is the country. We wouldn't expect the name of the United States or any other modern nation to be mentioned in the Bible—except for a few countries such as Egypt and Greece that still have their ancient names—because the Scriptures were written centuries ago. But we know that when the Eastern coalition armies begin their invasion of Israel for the Battle of Armageddon, they will be opposed by the Antichrist and a coalition of all the Western nations (Revelation 16:12–14). The United States will most likely be part of that coalition because it is a Western superpower. But the primary focus of end-time prophecies is on the Middle East and Europe. The rest of the world, including the United States, will be involved, but the spotlight is over there—not on the New World.

IS IT NOT FOOLISH TO SPECULATE ABOUT THE END TIMES?

We have to tread carefully in dealing with the prophecies concerning the end times. On the one hand, the Bible does make specific predictions about the end of the world. In addition, we are told to pay attention to these predictions, and when we see them come to pass, we know that our redemption is near (Matthew 24:33). On the other hand, we are warned against setting times and dates. Jesus said, "No one knows about that day or hour, not even the angels in heaven, nor the Son, but only the Father" (v. 36). We need to remind ourselves that everyone in the last two thousand years who has predicted a specific time for the end of the world has been wrong.

Ed Hindson, in his book *Final Signs*, develops a helpful paradigm for dealing with the end times. He delineates between the facts, the assumptions, and the speculations of biblical prophecies.

Facts. They are the clearly stated facts of prophetic revelation: Christ will return for his own; He will judge the world; there will be a time of great trouble on the earth at the end of the age; . . .

Assumptions. Factual prophecy only tells us so much and no more. Beyond that we must make certain assumptions. . . . for example, it is an assumption that Russia will invade Israel in the last days. Whether or not that is factual depends on the legitimacy of one's interpretation of Ezekiel's Magog prophecy (Ezekiel 38–39).

Speculations. These are purely calculated guesses based on assumptions.[2]

We do well to clearly identify our understanding of end times as either fact, assumption, or speculation.

WHAT ABOUT THE RIGHTS OF PALESTINIANS?

The Bible predicts the regathering of the Jewish people to Israel. This is where Jesus will establish his earthly kingdom. Right now, Israel exists as a State. But what about the rights of the displaced Palestinians who lost everything when Israel became a nation? Many theologians tend to ignore this most difficult question.

I was confronted with this matter as a college student in the late sixties. I had a good friend who was Palestinian and whose entire family lived in Jerusalem. He was a wonderful and vibrant Christian. But after the Six-Day War in 1967, when Israel took over all of Jerusalem, his family lost everything—their homes, their businesses, and their dignity. He had *nothing* good to say about the Jews. He would admit they were God's people and that they had a divine right to the land (Genesis 12), but he would repeatedly say, "I hate the Jews. I hate the Jews. I hate the Jews!"

For hours I listened to my friend's pain. There are displaced Palestinians in the church of which I am the senior pastor today. One of them has played the role of Jesus in our Easter play. Imagine that—an Arab playing the role of Jesus! This could only happen through the reconciliation that comes from the cross of Christ.

As Christians we ought to be interested in reconciling Jew and Palestinian. While we understand the divine right of Jews to Israel, that does not mean we ignore the needs and rights of Palestinians. We need to speak up for them as well.

IS THE ANTICHRIST ALIVE TODAY?

In the movie *The Final Conflict*, there is a scene in which a monk is praying to God. He is asking God to reveal to him the identity of the Antichrist so that he can be killed in order to guarantee the safety of Christ's return. Although the prayer is not based on the Bible—the Antichrist will be judged by God, not killed by a monk—the scene reflects the interest of many people in discussing the identity of the Antichrist.

Is the Antichrist alive today? He could be. The next great prophetic event is the rapture of the church. Following the Rapture there will be a seven-year period of tribulation during which the Antichrist will come to world power. This means that the Antichrist will have to be old enough at the time of the Rapture to exercise worldwide political power. In fact, I believe that many of the events that are predicted for the Tribulation will begin to take place prior to the Rapture. If we are living very close to the Rapture, then the Antichrist is alive.

SHOULD WE RESIST THE TREND TOWARD GLOBALISM?

Since coming to the United States in 1964, I have maintained a British passport because in some parts of the world it is easier to get access with a British passport. Several years ago I went to renew the passport, but instead of a British passport, I received a European-British passport. The front cover is similar to my previous passport; there is a coat of arms and, above it, the words "United Kingdom of Great Britain and Northern Ireland." But at the top are the words "European Community."

As we shift toward a global village, will all passports have the words "World Community" at the top? The Bible predicts this shift toward globalism, and we are well down the road in that direction. Should this be resisted? Some Christians think so. They see the trend as fundamentally evil since it paves the way for the Antichrist and his one-world government. Others see the trend as evil because it means the loss of national identity and individual freedoms. Some of these people are preparing for the end of the world by stockpiling ammunition and food and building bomb shelters.

I do not see the trend as fundamentally evil and therefore to be resisted. It is just a trend. In fact, it has wonderful advantages for Christians. As the world seems to become smaller and national boundaries become easier to cross, it opens up new possibilities for the gospel. In the changing world in which we live, we can either bemoan the changes or ask God to help us take advantage of them for the advancement of the gospel and the church.

WILL THE CHURCH GO THROUGH THE TRIBULATION?

There are at least three major views in regard to the church and the Tribulation. First, some teach that the church will not go through this turbulent period. Jesus will come and take the church out of the world to heaven—the event we call the Rapure. This view is called the pretribulation rapture of the church.

Second, others teach that the church will go through part of the Tribulation but not the entire seven-year period of time. The church will suffer persecution but will not have to endure the worst of the Tribution, the last three and a half years. Most who hold this view believe in a midtribulation rapture.

Third, some teach that the church will go through the entire Tribulation and that the so-called Rapture and the second coming of Jesus to establish his kingdom are the same event.

I believe that the church will be taken out of the world before the Great Tribulation. While there are some passages that might suggest otherwise, the bulk of biblical evidence seems to be on the side of a pretribulation rapture of the church. Consider the following biblical evidence:

1. The Bible promises protection for the church from the Great Tribulation.

> "Since you have kept my command to endure patiently, I will also keep you from the hour of trial that is going to come upon the whole world to test those who live on the earth."
>
> *Revelation 3:10*

2. Jesus encouraged his disciples to pray for deliverance from the Great Tribulation.

> "Be always on the watch, and pray that you may be able to escape all that is about to happen, and that you may be able to stand before the Son of Man."   *Luke 21:36*

3. The wrath of God that will be loosed during the Tribulation is for nonbelievers—not the church. The church is already in heaven with Jesus when these events occur (Revelation 19:7–9).

4. The focus of authority during the Tribulation will be Israel. The church is not even mentioned in the many tribulational prophecies found in the book of Revelation. I believe that is because the church is not on the earth—she is in heaven, having been delivered from the Tribulation by the Rapture.

SHOULD CHRISTIANS BE CONCERNED ABOUT NUCLEAR WEAPONS?

Since the invention of nuclear weapons, the entire world has lived with the possibility of quick and violent annihilation. At any moment it could all blow up. When we read the predictions found in the book of Revelation, some descriptions of future events have a remarkable parallel to the aftermath of an all-out nuclear war. If part of the world is going to be blown up anyway in some end-time holocaust, should Christians even care about this threat? After all, will we not be raptured and therefore not have to worry about these matters?

I believe that whatever happens in the future, we have a compelling responsibility to deal with the present situation. I remember years ago when Billy Graham went to the Soviet Union for an international conference on peace and the reduction of nuclear arms. Many Christians thought he had made a terrible mistake. People thought he was being manipulated by the Communist state. But Graham was committed to the idea that we need to reduce the number of nuclear weapons, or if possible, even eliminate them. I agree with that idea. To ignore the threat of nuclear weapons or not to care is not a responsible Christian option. We should work toward peace and the elimination of such weapons of indiscriminate mass destruction.

ARE COMPUTERS BAD?

I remember hearing years ago, when computers were first introduced, of a giant computer in Europe allegedly called "the Beast." I heard sermons preached against that computer. "We are in the last days," they declared. "We even have the computer that will set up the one-world economy." The message was clear: Computers are bad. In my research for this book I did my best to authenticate the story that "the Beast" exists. I did authenticate that there was a large computer in Europe, but I could not document that it was called "the Beast." Moreover, it was never designed for or capable of setting up a world-wide economic system.

The Bible predicts a shift toward a one-world economy. People will need to have the "mark of the Beast" to do business in this marketplace. It seems likely that computers will play a major role in the ongoing shift toward globalism, but that does *not* mean that computers are bad. Computers are technological, and technology is inherently neither morally good nor morally bad. The morality of technology is defined by how moral or immoral the human beings are who use it.

WHAT IS THE MOST SIGNIFICANT SIGN IN REGARD TO THE END OF THE WORLD?

The most significant sign—and the one that causes me to wonder whether we are indeed living in the last days—is the return of the Jews to Israel and the establishment of a Jewish state. In my opinion, the formation of the State of Israel in 1949 marked a significant event in the calendar of God and the march toward the end of the world.

Although this happened only about fifty years ago, biblical scholars had been predicting it for centuries. Their predictions were regarded as foolish and naïve. But they were right. I came across a booklet entitled *The Blessed Hope: Papers on the Lord's Coming and Connected Events*. It was published in 1901, but the lectures contained in it were delivered in 1879. The writer devotes an entire chapter to the return of the Jews to the land. He states, "There is nothing more certain from the word of God than that the Jews, who are now dispersed throughout the world, will be restored to their own land, . . ."[3] He adds,

> We thus see that God has not forgotten His covenant with Abraham (Gen. XVII 4–8); for while Israel failed in responsibility, and forfeited all claims upon God, He yet in faithfulness to His own word, in the wonder of His grace, will perform all He has spoken. And the time draws near when Israel, once again restored to their own land, "shall blossom and bud, and fill the face of the world with fruit" (Isaiah XXVII 6).[4]

Over a hundred years ago, this writer predicted that the return of the Jews "draws near." After nearly two thousand years of dispersion, the Jews have returned as a testimony to the miraculous power of God and the prophetic predictions of Scripture. For me, this is the most compelling sign indicating we may be living in the last days.

WILL JESUS RETURN BEFORE A.D. 2000?

This is the million-dollar question: Will Jesus return before A.D. 2000? As we approach this date and millennial fever rises to epidemic proportions, more and more people will be tempted to speculate that Jesus is likely to return when or before the next millennium begins. Remember, others have made such predictions in the past. They have named specific dates, and all these dates have come and gone and we still are looking for the return of Jesus. In other words, no one knows exactly when Jesus will return— whether before or after the turn of the millennium. But we *do* know that he will return.

Could Jesus return before A.D. 2000? This is a different question, and the answer is an absolute *yes!* Jesus could come at any moment. The stage of world history has been set. The specific players are in place. There are *no* more events prophesied in the Bible that have to take place before Jesus returns. He could come at any moment!

Chapter 12

HOW THEN SHOULD WE LIVE?

In this book I have focused and expanded on three major ideas.

1. The Bible predicts that Jesus Christ is coming again to the earth to set up his kingdom.

2. The Bible predicts in detail many of the events that will precede Jesus' coming. These include the rapture of the church; the Great Tribulation; the rise of the Antichrist; the establishment of a one-world government, economy, and church; and the final Battle of Armageddon.

3. The events occurring today have incredible likeness to the events predicted in the Bible. The current situation in the world more closely parallels the end times as predicted than any other time since Jesus ascended to heaven.

In light of these three realities, how, then, should we live?

This is *not* a question frequently asked by people interested in end-time prophecies. I have listened to dozens of sermons and watched many movies on the subject, and very few people look seriously at how we should live in light of the imminent coming of Jesus. Unfortunately, many are only interested in the latest Bible interpretations and speculations. They are not much interested in the practical, day-to-day implications of Bible prophecy. Yet, as we study the prophetic passages dealing with the end of the world, we see that nearly all of them are accompanied by clear instruction as to how we should live *today*.

SOME ADVICE FROM JESUS

What if we were able to go to heaven and have a personal conversation with Jesus about his going back to the earth and the end of the world? That would be a most fascinating dialogue. What would Jesus say as we got ready to return to the earth? What would he say about how we should live as we eagerly await his return? We do not have to speculate on that. While Jesus lived on the earth he gave specific instructions to his disciples about how they should live. That discourse is recorded in Matthew 23–25. It is an extended conversation about the signs of his coming and the end of the world.

In this book we have looked at chapter 24 in great detail as regards the last days. But most of Jesus' discourse is devoted to the matter of how we are to live in light of the end of the world. Jesus spends more time on this topic than he does enumerating the specific signs. In Matthew 25 he relates three parables to inform us of our responsibility while we wait for the end of the age.[1]

1. *The Parable of the Ten Virgins: Be Prepared for the Coming of the Lord.*

The story told in Matthew 25:1–13 concerns ten virgins who are waiting for the bridegroom to arrive for the wedding ceremony and the wedding feast. Each of the women had a lamp. Five of the virgins are called "wise" because they brought an additional supply of oil for their lamps. Five are called "foolish" because they did not bring extra oil. When the bridegroom was delayed, the women all became drowsy and fell asleep. Finally the virgins awoke. All the lamps now needed more oil—but the foolish virgins did not have any. They were told to go and buy more oil, and while they were away, the bridegroom arrived. The five women missed the wedding feast.

Jesus concluded the story with a warning: "Therefore keep watch, because you do not know the day or the hour" (v. 13).

The message of Jesus in this story is clear. First, we do not know when Jesus will come. It could be today or tomorrow or this year or next year. It could be before A.D. 2000, or it could be after that. Second, Jesus could come at any moment. The early church anticipated that Jesus could come in their lifetime. We should have that same sense of expectation. Third, we should be ready for Jesus' return. We don't want to be like the foolish virgins who were not prepared.

2. *The Parable of the Ten Talents: Be Good Stewards of What God Has Given You.*

Verses 14–30 tell the story of a rich landowner who went on a journey and entrusted his property to three men. He gave the first man five talents—a monetary unit of those times. To the second man he gave two talents, and to the third, one talent. During the owner's absence the man with five talents worked hard and gained another five talents. The man with two talents also worked hard and gained two more. But the man with one talent dug a hole in the ground and hid the money.

When the property owner returned, he met with the three men. He was very pleased with the first two and commended both. "Well done, good and faithful servant!" he said. "You have been faithful with a few things; I will put you in charge of many things. Come and share your master's happiness!" (vv. 21, 23). But the owner was not pleased with the third man. The last man had not done anything with his talent. The owner called him a "wicked, lazy servant" (v. 26); he took that lone talent and gave it to the first man. He then threw the servant "outside, into the darkness, where there will be weeping and gnashing of teeth" (v. 30).

The truth revealed in this story is that God has given each person "talents"—that is, something to put to use. One day when Jesus returns, he will judge our stewardship of the resources he has given us. It is our responsibility to invest our resources in strategic ways to advance the interests of the master—God. If we are faithful as good stewards of these resources, we will be commended by God and will be put in charge of many things in the earthly kingdom of Jesus Christ.

What are we doing with the material resources God has given us? This is the compelling question raised by the parable. Are we hoarding the resources like the third man, or are we investing and multiplying our resources for the purposes of the Master? I am concerned that when it comes to money and material things, we live as if there is no eternity and no hope of the coming of Jesus. We are self-indulgent and hoard our resources for our own benefit rather than investing them for kingdom purposes. We believe in the Second Coming. We believe that our stewardship will be judged. But we actually live as if God did not exist and Jesus was in fact not coming. I would say that makes us *eschatalogical atheists!*

3. *The Sheep and the Goats: True Faith Is Authenticated in Compassion for the Poor.*

The parable told in verses 31–46 concerns the judgment when Jesus comes to separate the sheep—his followers—from the goats—nonbelievers. The focus of the parable is on the criteria by which Jesus will make his judgments. People will be measured by what they did for the hungry, the thirsty, the homeless (the "stranger"), the naked, the sick, and the prisoners (vv. 34–36). Those who take care of these people will be invited into the kingdom. Those who ignored them will be "cursed" and thrown into "the eternal fire prepared for the devil and his angels" (v. 41).

This is a disturbing story and one difficult to understand. The major truth is both mysterious and discomforting: When we minister to the poor, we are ministering to Jesus. When Jesus judges the goats, he declares, "I was hungry and you gave me nothing to eat, I was thirsty and you gave me nothing to drink, I was a stranger and you did not invite me in, I needed clothes and you did not clothe me, I was sick and in prison and you did not look after me" (vv. 42–43). Those receiving this rebuke are shocked. "We never saw you that way," they said. The implication is that if they had seen Jesus having these needs, they would have undoubtedly responded more favorably.

The point Jesus makes is that they did indeed see him in the cause of the poor, but ignored him. "I tell you the truth," he said, "whatever you did not do for one of the least of these, you did not do for me" (v. 45). Jesus is saying that when we give food to the hungry, we are giving it to the Lord himself. Likewise, when we give water to the thirsty. When we shelter the homeless, we are sheltering Jesus. When we clothe the naked, we are clothing Jesus. When we visit the sick and prisoners, we are visiting Jesus. To touch and care for the needs of others is to touch and care for Jesus. To ignore them is to ignore Jesus.

I must confess that I do not understand the theology of this statement. How can Jesus be present in the poor? How can single acts of love toward the poor be, in fact, simple acts of love for Jesus? I do not know the answer to these questions, but I do know that we are to live out our faith with acts of love for "the least of these"—and when Jesus comes, we will be judged according to these deeds.

While I do not understand this truth, I have on many occasions experienced it. Many years ago we decided as a church to try to demonstrate love and care for people who are HIV-positive. We concluded that these people were some of the most alienated, forgotten, and discriminated against people in our community. We concluded that if Jesus were bodily present in our city, he would be hanging out with HIV-positive people and their families. Over the years I have personally walked with many HIV-positive people through the dark and lonely battle that eventually took their lives. In the midst of our journey together, I have discovered the presence of Jesus in an inexplicable and supernatural way.

I think of one man we will call Bill. Bill was a successful businessman in the community, with a respected family. All his life he had struggled with his sexuality and had a private life that few people knew about. He eventually became HIV-positive, and then it turned to full-blown AIDS. It was a difficult journey. One day I spent hours with him as he poured out his entire story to me. We cried and hugged and prayed. He shared all the details of that story with his family, who forgave him and stood by him in the last month of his life.

I was with Bill the night he died. He was in a darkened room in the hospice ward of a local hospital. His body had been ravaged by the disease, and he was a shell of what he had been. His eyes were sunken, and he was unconscious. During the night I read every passage in the Bible dealing with heaven. It was in many ways a strange scene: A darkened room. Stark and simple furniture. A dying man. The Bible. The hope of heaven.

As I sat by Bill's bed, knowing that he was headed to heaven, I had the strange sensation that I was sitting in the presence of Jesus. I felt that Jesus was present through Bill in an inexplicable but powerful way—more real than being among thousands in the pews on a Sunday morning, more real than in the visible public ministry of our church. Jesus—present in "the least of these" (Matthew 25:45).

When we face Jesus in judgment, we will be reckoned by how we treated the needy people God brought our way. Jesus is not teaching a way of salvation by social responsibility. We are saved exclusively by faith. Rather, he is teaching that a *saving* faith is one that is translated into action. Too many of us evangelical Christians have completely lost the social implications of the gospel. Jesus is all around us in the hungry, naked, homeless, sick, and imprisoned. Will we continue to ignore them and Jesus? The prospect of Jesus' return ought to motivate us to action in behalf of the marginalized people in our communities.

LIVE WITH ETERNITY IN VIEW

"You also must be ready, because the Son of Man will come at an hour when you do not expect him." *Luke 12:40*

There are two compelling realities about life and eternity. First, life is brief and uncertain. The Bible is full of warnings about the brevity of life. Life is like the grass that is here today and gone tomorrow (Psalm 102:11). It is like a flower that blossoms one day and withers the next (Psalm 103:15–16). We are told not to "boast about tomorrow"—about our grandiose plans (Proverbs 27:1). Second, Jesus could come at any moment. The Bible admonishes us to be ready at any moment for his return. We are to live each day confronted by the reality of eternity.

In my teens I knew other Christian teenagers whose parents often put them on a heavy guilt trip. Before these teenagers would go out for the evening, their parents would say something like this: "Now, remember that you are a Christian. Don't go places you should not go—like the movies. If you do go there and Jesus comes back, he will not know where to look for you!" I look back at that advice and laugh. It is theological error through and through. Jesus is God and knows everything; he would certainly know where to look for us if he returned. But there is an element of compelling truth in their statement. We are to live each day and each moment of each day with an awareness that Jesus could come at any time. Such an awareness will affect how we live, what we say, what we do, and where we go.

> Dear friends, now we are children of God, and what we will be has not yet been made known. But we know that when he appears, we shall be like him, for we shall see him as he is. Everyone who has this hope in him purifies himself, just as he is pure. *1 John 3:2–3*

Many people in my church are wearing a wristband with the letters *W.W.J.D.* They stand for "What Would Jesus Do?" It is a reminder throughout the day to keep asking the question: "What would Jesus do" and whatever it is—do it! Perhaps we should develop another wristband: *W.I.J.C.T.* "What If Jesus Came Today?" How would I live? What would I do? Where would I go? What goals would I want to accomplish? This is precisely how we should live—with eternity in view.

DO NOT FORGET THE CREATION MANDATE

The Bible predicts massive environmental changes for the worse as the world nears an end. It predicts the destruction of grasslands and forests, the poisoning of waters and oceans, the vast destruction of wildlife and sea creatures, global warming and major changes in the seasons. These trends do not relieve us of the responsibility to care for our environment and do all we can to protect it. The inevitable deterioration of the physical world does not excuse us from our present biblical responsibilities.

At the Creation, human beings were given specific responsibilities for the environment. God told Adam and Eve to "fill the earth and subdue it" and work the garden of Eden and "take care of it" (Genesis 1:28; 2:15). All the earth belongs to God (Psalm 24:1), and all of creation reflects his glory (Psalm 19:1). We are stewards of that creation, and as such, we protect God's glory as revealed in the natural world.

As Christians who look for the coming of Jesus we too often ignore our responsibilities to the creation. On the one hand, we may develop a fatalism based on our understanding of the end times. "Things are getting worse. The environment is being destroyed," we reason. "It's all part of the plan. Therefore I have no responsibility to resist the trend." The apostle Paul states that since the Fall, the creation has been "groaning," longing for deliverance (Romans 8:22). But this deterioration does not absolve us of the responsibility to do what we can with what we have to protect the environment. On the other hand, we may ignore the environment because we are afraid of worshiping the creation rather than the Creator. We are afraid that in protecting the environment we will develop a distorted view of the creation. However, genuine care for the creation is in fact the working out of our faith through obedience to the word of the God who created the world.[2]

FACING THE NUCLEAR THREAT

The descriptions of the destruction of human life and the environment predicted in the Bible for the end times have great similarity with the consequences of nuclear explosions. Many people believe that there will be a major nuclear war during the Tribulation. Because of this, some have taken a casual attitude toward the threat of nuclear war. They feel that because the church will be taken out of the world before these events occur, we need not be concerned about the problem of nuclear weapons.

I believe that view is fatally flawed. Nothing in the Bible precludes the possibility of nuclear war occurring before the Rapture and the Tribulation. In other words, to believe that nuclear war will not occur until the Tribulation gives a false sense of security. The truth is, we live every day with the possibility that someone, somewhere, will either accidentally or deliberately push the button and wreak havoc on the earth.

The existence and proliferation of nuclear weapons should be a concern of every Christian because of their potential to bring mass destruction of life and the natural world. What can Christians do? First, we can pray and encourage the reduction and elimination of such weapons. Second, we can preach and model the gospel of reconciliation that reduces the tensions that lead to war. Jesus came to reconcile sinners to God and to each other across ethnic, social, racial, gender, and cultural boundaries. At a time when ethnic cleansing, tribal warfare, and religious hatred is all too present, we desperately need to proclaim the gospel in word and deed—a gospel of reconciliation.

GOD IS THE GOD OF HUMAN HISTORY

In the midst of a changing world and the march toward Armageddon, one thing remains certain: God is in control. God is the Lord of history, and all of history is marching toward the second coming of Jesus Christ. The prophet Daniel received many visions about future events. From them he understood that God is in control and that these predictions, though pertaining to ages to come, had immediate implications for his own life. These are God's last words to Daniel after the prophet had received some fearful revelations about the future.

> "As for you, go your way till the end. You will rest, and then at the end of the days you will rise to receive your allotted inheritance." *Daniel 12:13*

"Go your way till the end." Because God is the God of human history and he is in control, we have a responsibility to keep on seeking him and doing what he has called us to do. Some people get consumed by end-time prophecies. They study and read. They learn and speculate. But they forget that our future hope should drive us to *serve* God in the present.

"You will rest." Our hope does not lie in any political system of this world. Here on earth we will continue to struggle in a world of increasing chaos. But our permanent dwelling is not here. We are aliens and strangers, just passing through. Our rest is in eternity.

"You will rise to receive your allotted inheritance." Our reward is in heaven. If we belong to God through faith in Christ, we are guaranteed an eternal dwelling and will be judged and rewarded according to the way we lived down here (Matthew 25).

AM I READY FOR THE COMING OF JESUS?

If Jesus were to return today, would I be ready to meet him? The Bible teaches that when Jesus comes for the church, only those who are believers will rise to meet him in the clouds and spend the rest of eternity with him (1 Thessalonians 4:13–18). I must ask you, "Do you know Jesus Christ personally? If he were to return today, do you know whether you will be taken to heaven? If you were to die today, are you certain you would go to heaven?"

Human beings were created in the image of God to enjoy an intimate and personal relationship with him (Genesis 1:27). Adam and Eve enjoyed that intimate relationship with their Creator, but then disobeyed him and were driven from Paradise. Because of their disobedience, all human beings are sinners and are separated from God (Romans 3:10–18, 23). The holiness of God demands perfection as the prerequisite for a relationship, and it requires punishment for sin. For human beings this presents a double dilemma: We can never measure up to God's standard of perfection, and God's perfection requires that our sin be punished with death (Romans 6:23).

But the good news of the gospel is that God himself acted to correct the problem. He sent his only Son to die as our substitute. When Jesus died, he suffered the penalty of our sin on our behalf (Hebrews 10:10, 12). We can be forgiven of our sin and declared as righteous through the death, burial, and resurrection of Jesus Christ (Romans 5:1–2). This forgiveness and acceptance by God come through personal faith and commitment to Jesus Christ.

> Yet to all who received him, to those who believed in his name, he gave the right to become children of God.
>
> *John 1:12*

We must do two things for salvation: believe and receive. We must believe that we are sinners separated from God. We must believe that Jesus Christ is God's son. We must believe that Jesus died, was buried, and rose again as my substitute. Second, we must receive Jesus as our personal Lord and Savior.

I made this decision in Belfast, Northern Ireland, when I was eleven years old. I knelt by my bed one night and prayed a prayer similar to the following:

> Dear God, I know I am a sinner. Please forgive me. I believe that Jesus died and rose again for me. Come into my life, Lord Jesus. I receive you as my Lord and Savior. I want to follow you for the rest of my life.

That prayer was my first step in a lifelong journey of following Jesus. It was the most important step. If Jesus were to come today or if I were to die today, I *know* I would go to heaven. Have you settled the issue of your eternal destiny?

If you are prepared for Jesus' return, what are you doing to share the gospel with those who do not know him? How are you helping to give the Good News to people in your community and around the world? When Jesus ascended to heaven, the disciples stood gazing into the sky. Two angels appeared to them and said, "Men of Galilee, . . . why do you stand here looking into the sky?" (Acts 1:11). Jesus had given them instructions just before he left: They were to wait in Jerusalem for the Holy Spirit, then they were to be Jesus' witnesses "in Jerusalem, and in all Judea and Samaria, and to the ends of the earth" (v. 8). I fear that we often gaze in the sky and forget the mission: To get the gospel out to everybody in the world.

HEADLIGHTS IN THE SNOW

A group of people in our church has adopted some of the homeless people in our city—people who live year-round under the bridges downtown. This group takes a hot meal to these homeless each evening and provide basic necessities when asked. The church people simply love them and have cultivated a relationship with them.

I went with one of the men to visit a man we'll call Fred. It was the middle of winter, the snow was blowing, and the windchill was 30 degrees below zero. We drove downtown. We walked along an isolated path to the bridge. In the center of the bridge was a cardboard box covered with a bunch of blankets. Fred did not want to eat the hot meal in his box. "It attracts mice and rats," he said. So we went back to the car and sat with Fred while he ate the meal.

Fred had been living at the bridge for more than three years. He was alert and intelligent. He was a skilled tradesman but had chosen to live in the cardboard box. He called it his condo. "Great advantages," he said. "No heating or lighting bills, and the IRS doesn't know where I am." I enjoyed our conversation. When he was through eating, Fred made his way back down the path and into the darkness of that winter night.

It was snowing as I drove home. I noticed an unusual phenomenon that I had never seen before. The way the snow was coming down caused lights to cast their beam straight up into the sky. Streetlights, car lights—all pointed straight up. The sky was filled with lights pointing upward.

The scene is really an illustration of how many of us live. We keep pointing our lights to the sky waiting for the coming of Jesus Christ. This is important. But underneath the bridges we cross and all around us are people who need to be illuminated by the lights we carry. We need to keep looking for Jesus to come, but we must never forget that we have responsibilities until he comes. Let us spread the light around.

NOTES

CHAPTER 1: The End of the World as We Know It

1. Gerald O. Barney with Jane Blewett and Kristen R. Barney, *Global 2000 Revisited: What Shall We Do?* A Report on the Critical Issues of the Twenty-first Century Prepared for the 1993 Parliament of the World's Religions (New York: Millennium Institute, 1993).

2. Ibid.

3. Otto Nathan and Heinz Norden, eds. *Einstein on Peace* (New York: Schocken, 1968), 376.

4. Norman Moss, *Men Who Play God: The Story of the H-Bomb and How the World Came to Live with It* (New York: Penguin Books, 1968), 1.

5. Jeannie Peterson, ed. *The Aftermath: The Human and Ecological Consequences of Nuclear War* (New York: Pantheon Books, 1993), 16–17.

6. Avner Cohen and Steven Lee, eds. *Nuclear Weapons and the Future of Humanity* (Totowa, N.Y.: Rowman & Allanheld, 1986), 9.

7. Cohen and Lee, *Nuclear Weapons and the Future of Humanity,* 1.

8. Peterson, *The Aftermath,* 76, 90.

9. Ibid.

10. Ibid.

11. Ibid., 1.

12. See Gillian Paterson, *Love in a Time of AIDS: Women, Health and the Challenge of HIV* (Geneva: WCC Publications, 1996).

13. Seymour M. Hersh, *Chemical and Biological Warfare: America's Hidden Arsenal* (Indianapolis: Bobbs-Merrill, 1968), 68.

14. Russell Chandler, *Racing Toward 2001: The Forces Shaping America's Religious Future* (Grand Rapids: Zondervan, 1992), 69–81.

15. Barney, Blewett, and Barney, *Global 2000 Revisited: What Shall We Do?*

CHAPTER 2: The Coming of Jesus: When and How?

1. Louis Berkhof, *Systematic Theology* (Grand Rapids: Eerdmans, 1969), 129.

2. *The Wall Street Journal*, 4 September 1996, 1.

CHAPTER 3: Israel: God's Focus for the Future

1. Paul Johnson, *A History of the Jews* (New York: Harper & Row, 1987), 3.

2. Ibid., 4.

3. Ibid., 519.

4. Eva Fleischner, ed. *Auschwitz: Beginning of a New Era? Reflections of the Holocaust* (New York: Ktav Publishing House, 1977), 9–10.

5. See Johnson, *A History of the Jews*, 522–25.

6. Ibid., 527.

CHAPTER 4: The End of the World According to Daniel

1. An interesting footnote to what was a wonderful time: When we were about halfway through, I noticed the course manager coming toward us in a cart. He had someone with him. I thought, *What in the world have we done? We're going to be thrown off the golf course.* They pulled up, and the manager said, "This is so-and-so from the *Grand Rapids Press.* He is doing an article on what people do on Thanksgiving Day. Could he take your photograph?" The next day the front page of the newspaper had a beautiful picture of my dad, with his Irish cap, putting on the seventeenth green. The first time he played golf—front page of the *Grand Rapids Press!*

2. Much of the following is adapted from Ed Dobson, *Daniel: Making Right Choices* (Grand Rapids: Revell, 1994).

3. Richard Mayne, *The Community of Europe: Past, Present and Future* (New York: W. W. Norton, 1963), 28–29.

4. See Uwe Kitzinger, *The European Common Market and Community* (New York: Barnes and Noble, 1967).

CHAPTER 5: The Emerging New World Order

1. Mikhail Gorbachev, "U.S.S.R. Arms Reduction," *Vital Speeches of the Day*, 1 February 1989, 230. Delivered at the United Nations, New York, 7 December 1988: quoted by Ed Hindson, *The New World Order* (Wheaton, Ill.: Victor Books, 1991), 14.

2. Ed Hindson, *Final Signs* (Eugene, Ore.: Harvest House, 1996), 21.

3. Nate Krupp, *The Omega Generation* (Harrison, Ark.: New Leaf Press, 1977), 78.

4. Leland M. Goodrich and Anne P. Simons, *The United Nations and the Maintenance of International Peace and Security* (Washington, D.C.: Brookings Institution, 1955), 635.

5. Ibid., 636.

6. Salem Kirban, *The Rise of Antichrist* (Huntingdon Valley, Pa.: Salem Kirban, Inc., 1978), 172–73.

7. Robert Ellis Smith, "The True Terror Is in the Land," *New York Times Magazine,* 8 September 1996, sect. 6, 59.

8. Ibid.

9. Quoted in ibid.

10. Hindson, *The New World Order,* 69.

11. Gerald O. Barney with Jane Blewett and Kristen R. Barney, *Global 2000 Revisited: Overview.* A Report on the Critical Issues of the Twenty-first Century Prepared for the 1993 Parliament of the World's Religions (New York: Millennium Institute, 1993).

12. Ibid.

CHAPTER 6: The Rise and Fall of the Antichrist

1. Thomas Ice and Timothy Demy, *The Antichrist and His Kingdom* (Eugene, Ore.: Harvest House, 1996), 9–10.

CHAPTER 8: Armageddon: The Mother of All Battles

1. *Merriam Webster's Collegiate Dictionary, Tenth Edition* (Springfield, Mass.: Merriam-Webster, 1993), 63.

2. Quote supplied by the Anti-Defamation League of the B'nai B'rith and quoted by John Hagee, *Beginning of the End* (Nashville: Thomas Nelson, 1996), 144.

3. Ed Hindson, *The New World Order* (Wheaton, Ill.: Victor Books, 1991), 138.

4. This view is also suggested by Ed Hindson in *Final Signs* (Eugene, Ore.: Harvest House, 1996), 134–35.

CHAPTER 9: The Millennium

1. Harold Willmington, *The King Is Coming* (Wheaton, Ill.: Tyndale House, 1973), 206–8.

2. Hal Lindsey, *The Late Great Planet Earth* (Grand Rapids: Zondervan, 1970), 174.

3. Willmington, *The King Is Coming,* 225.

CHAPTER 10: Fifty Remarkable Events Pointing Toward the End

1. Quoted by Ed Hindson, *The New World Order* (Wheaton, Ill.: Victor Books, 1991), 71.

2. Ibid., 81–83. Hindson gives a thorough overview of the long tradition of identifying current events with biblical prophecy.

3. Edgar C. Whisenant, *88 Reasons Why the Rapture Will Be in 1988* (Nashville: World Bible Society, 1988).

4. Thomas Ice and Timothy Demy, *The Last Days Temple* (Eugene, Ore.: Harvest House, 1996), 30.

5. Ibid.

6. Ibid.

7. As quoted in *World Watch* 9, no. 4 (July–August 1996), 21.

CHAPTER 11: Top Ten List of Most Frequently Asked Questions About the End Times

1. Jack Van Impe, *2001: On the Edge of Eternity* (Dallas: Word Books, 1996), 165–84.

2. Ed Hindson, *Final Signs* (Eugene, Ore.: Harvest House, 1996), 36–37.

3. E. D., *The Blessed Hope: Papers on the Lord's Coming* (London: A. S. Rouse, 1901), 48.

4. Ibid., 58.

CHAPTER 12: How Then Should We Live?

1. Some Bible scholars believe that these parallels only apply to those who are alive during the Tribulation and kingdom age and therefore do not concern us today. Whether or not this is true, I believe that the core teaching is very applicable for us as we wait for the coming of Jesus Christ.

2. For more information see the magazine *Green Cross,* published by the Christian Society of the Green Cross, 101 East Lancaster Avenue, Wynnewood, PA 19096.